Eating
Dr. King's Dinner

A Memoir of the Movement
1963-1966

Chuck Fager

Kimo Press

Copyright © 2005 by Chuck Fager.
All Rights Reserved.

ISBN No. 0-945177-24-0

Front cover photo © by
John F. Phillips.
videoeve@rogers.com
Used by permission.

Kimo Press
P.O. Box 1344
Fayetteville NC 28302
www.kimopress.com

For my children,
And grandchildren,
Because I wanted you to know.

And For Wendy,
Better late than never.

Chapter One
Eating Dr. King's Dinner

I

That morning, I was too tense to eat. Keyed up and ready, my thoughts were full of armies marching to battle.

It was February 1, 1965. I was part of a nonviolent "army" – or at least a battalion – set to march in Selma, Alabama that day. Our objective, the territory we hoped to occupy, was downtown, the Dallas County jail; we planned to capture it by getting arrested.

I had been in Selma less than a month. Perhaps because I was raised on military bases, comparing the movement to an army was came easily to me: Dr. King was the general; I, white and fresh from college in Colorado, was a private, a grunt.

Although our commander had just been awarded the Nobel Peace Prize, his ragtag force was ready for combat and bent on conquest. For us, victory meant nothing less than the overthrow of centuries of black exclusion from public office, the ballot, and the jury box in most of the American South.

Of course, the military parallel is wildly inexact: for one thing, we aimed at a bloodless coup; more mundanely, even in 1965 a real army private earned considerably more than my pittance of $25 per week. One didn't join the movement to carry a gun, or get rich.

On the other hand, the comparison was not wholly fanciful; after all, both groups demanded real discipline, and suffered real casualties.

Our ostensible destination that morning was the Dallas County Courthouse downtown, to renew a demand that the county voting rolls be opened to all its citizens. No one expected to get that far, however. Everybody knew we wanted to provoke arrests: the staff knew it, black Selmians knew it. The cops knew it too; and presumably the Klan, along with some of the people who kept sending Dr. King death threats, threats that came in practically every day, by mail, phone, and other media. I had seen a few of the threatening letters, and knew that many of them were quite credible.

In the years since Dr. King's murder, I have been bemusedly tolerant of the plethora of conspiracy theories offered in explanation, tending to believe and disbelieve them all, in equal measure. The CIA? The Klan? The Mafia? A redneck hit squad? A lone bigot? All are plausible. Yet I'm evenhandedly skeptical too, because while one of the conspiracies finally succeeded, I know well enough that there were numerous others which were foiled only by chance, by timely police intervention, or –

– or, well, because someone like me was walking near Dr. King at just the right moment, and blocked a sniper's aim.

II

That was one of my early tasks as a rookie civil rights worker: to stay close to Dr. King when we filed through the Selma streets. There were three or four of us who shared this duty, and we kept him pretty much surrounded.

We were the point men, his bodyguards. Unarmed, of course, and in my case at least, no great physical threat to any direct assailant. But without weapons and muscle, how were we supposed to provide protection?

Simple: our bodies were visual obstructions, blocking the aim of any sniper crouched on nearby rooftops, trying to draw a bead on Dr. King through the scope of a high-powered rifle.

The job was explained to me by big James Orange, who had been around the movement a lot longer. I grasped its function at once. But I also had a question: What if the sniper fired anyway, hoping for a lucky shot, and hit me instead?

James Orange answered my query first with a characteristically broad, hearty grin. Then he shrugged, slapped me on the shoulder and said, "Hey, don't worry about it, Chuck. If you get killed, we promise – Dr. King will preach at your funeral!"

"Hey, thanks, Jim," I retorted, "that makes me feel *so* much better." But the comeback took a couple seconds longer to come up with than I wanted.

Five e years later, researching my book *Selma 1965*, I found references to a police report which said that on one of our marches there may well have been a rifleman on a rooftop, poised to do just what I was there to prevent. Dr. King, it turned out, learned of this much sooner; he had spoken calmly about it to reporters a few days later.

Reading about the report made the hairs on the back of my neck stand up. But I wasn't really surprised.

III

Barely nibbling breakfast that morning, frightened and exhilarated at the same time, I donned my movement uniform: still-stiff denim overalls, a matching jacket and, incongruously, a yarmulke. Another staff member, who understood the importance of Jewish support to the movement, had passed them out to us not long before. Knowing little about either Judaism or black Baptist Christianity, it was all the same to me. Properly decked out, I headed across town for Brown Chapel AME Church.

Brown Chapel was red brick, with two squat steeples. It sat on Sylvan Street in the middle of the George Washington Carver Homes, Selma's neat, generally well-kept black housing project. People were milling around on the steps, and inside the benches were full.

There was a "mass meeting" underway, led by various key staffers, to get everybody into the right frame of mind for the day's events. Even at that early hour of the morning, the crowd was ready; and the intensity and fervor of such meetings are beyond my powers to describe. The elements were basic and familiar: preaching, praying, singing, clapping; but the combination, in those days, in that place, produced an uplifting energy that was unique, unforgettable, and overwhelming. I have known nothing quite like it, before or since.

Our marching orders were boomed from the pulpit, along with reminders of the need for strict nonviolent discipline, and reassurances that going to jail or being hurt in the cause of justice was nothing to be ashamed of. There was tension in the church, because we knew anything could happen; but there wasn't the cold fear I knew on other days, when violence hung in the air like heavy mist.

After a concluding prayer and a round of "We Shall Overcome," we were soon lining up outside, watching our breath in the chilly morning air, then stepping off, clapping and singing, headed up Sylvan Street toward the courthouse, about ten blocks away.

As planned, I ended up near Dr. King, at the head of the column. We hadn't gone far, barely a block, before we were stopped by a white man in a dark business suit and a fedora hat, standing in the middle of the street with his hands in his pockets. This was Wilson Baker, Selma's Public Safety Director. Baker was a good and smart man, a worthy opponent to Dr. King. If we had faced him alone in Selma, it's a fair guess that he would have routed us.

Baker would have beat the movement not with force, but with brains. He was a disciple of Police Chief Laurie Pritchett, his counterpart in Albany, Georgia, who had outsmarted and outmaneuvered a vigorous protest campaign there three years earlier.

IV

Albany's movement had had everything: marches, protests, new freedom songs, and many arrests. Dr. King had come too, and even faced jail. But in the movement's still-fresh folklore, Albany was the archetype of disaster.

This was because Laurie Pritchett had figured out how to handle the pack of Yankee reporters who showed up wherever Dr. King entered the fray. They swarmed into southern towns with their cameras, microphones, notebooks and expectations. Above all, they expected to see crude redneck cops and club-wielding sheriffs beating up and brutalizing peaceable, noble Negroes.

Pritchett understood the reporters' stereotypes, and was careful not to reinforce them. Instead, he spoke politely to the reporters, and made sure that when his police arrested the marchers, they did so quietly and without fanfare. (There were, of course, stories of beatings inside the jail. But those happened out of sight; Pritchett stoutly denied them, and the allegations could not be confirmed.) Instead of officially-sponsored mayhem, what Pritchett served up looked like a model of seemingly civilized southern restraint, upholding law and order against a disorderly crowd of black insurgents.

Pritchett's strategy succeeded brilliantly, on two fronts: with no exciting violence to film and write about, the Yankee reporters were thrown off-stride, and quickly becoming bored, soon moved on to some other, more exciting event. As they did so, the divisions in the local black community – there were always divisions in local black communities – flared up into recriminations and sapped the movement's morale and momentum. The defeat of the Albany campaign made Pritchett something of a hero to many southern officials. He traveled the region giving speeches about how he had whipped the agitators and sent Dr. King packing. Among his hearers, none had been more attentive than Selma's Wilson Baker.

Baker had the Pritchett mild-mannered strategy cold, right down to the non-threatening title of Public Safety Director he had chosen himself, and his civilian-style suit and fedora, which matched and blended with Dr. King's typical attire. As the march approached, it was evident that if King was now determined to get arrested, Baker was ready to accommodate him – but he would also make sure that the hovering crowd of reporters saw nothing more exciting in the process than a lot of colored people milling around outside the back entrance to the three-story City Hall, where the city and county jails occupied the upstairs floors.

For his part, Dr. King had learned from Albany too, and he planned both to outmaneuver Baker and use him at the same time. He wanted Baker to make the arrests, because King would feel safer in Baker's city jail. And at the same time, Baker's own restraint, however successful with the Yankee media, would work against him with a crucial local constituency.

Selma, fortunately for us, was not Albany. Here, for all his outward composure, Baker lacked Laurie Pritchett's control of the situation in white Selma, as we knew well enough. In particular, Baker couldn't afford to let us get past him to the courthouse, because the Dallas County Sheriff, Jim Clark, was waiting there.

V

Sheriff Clark was a walking stereotype: a tough-talking, head-cracking Deep South lawman, who had no patience with civil rights protests, or with Baker's "coddling" of agitators. Further, besides his deputies, Clark was backed by a volunteer posse. The posse had first earned notoriety for helping beat up and banish labor organizers in various parts of this so-called "right to work" state. Just the year before, they had been turned loose on earlier civil rights marches, with predictably bloody results. But Dr. King was not there then, and the beatings attracted only minor outside notice.

All of us who were marching had seen the possemen on earlier days, hefting long unpainted homemade billy clubs, and looking anxious to get at us. Their uniform consisted mainly of various shades of ill-fitting khaki work clothes, and white plastic hard hats bearing small metallic foil "Posse" stickers. Most possemen also had a large pistol hanging from one hip, and an electric cattle prod dangling from the other. These latter were battery-filled cylinders, like overlong flashlights, with metal prongs at one end. The cattle prods produced a nasty shock; the longest ones were said to sear bare flesh.

No question about it: the posse looked feral and dangerous. Compared to them, Baker's black-uniformed policemen seemed like pillars of professional restraint, protecting us from the sheriff's troops more than they were protecting white Selma from us.

When Clark and the posse broke up the marches a year earlier, they had gotten away with it. Then in November, 1964 a young appliance salesman named Joe Smitherman won a very close mayoral election by promising to bring in new industries and jobs. But Northern companies weren't interested in Clark's version of law and order, so Smitherman hired Baker to polish up the town's image.

Ever since, Baker and Clark had been jockeying for control of the city's streets and image. When Dr. King announced his plans to come to Selma, their struggle was ratcheted up several notches.

With the usual retinue of reporters and cameras in his wake, Dr. King had been playing on this tension and planned to raise it carefully but relentlessly to a fever pitch. That would keep the Yankee press interested, and maintain movement solidarity. The fact that on this February morning the tension between the two law enforcement units was almost palpable suggested that Dr. King's plan was working at least as well as Baker's.

VI

Our earlier marches had stayed on the sidewalks. This time, though, we were proceeding brazenly down the middle of Sylvan Street. That made us a parade, and a parade without a permit. Baker couldn't ignore this challenge. It would look to Clark's supporters as if he was giving in to the country's most notorious agitator, and bolster the sheriff's contention that white

Selma was being sold out to lawless black invaders.

Baker followed the script, testily reminding Dr. King that he didn't have a permit, and warned that if we didn't return to the sidewalk immediately, he'd have to arrest us.

Taking his cue, Dr. King quietly demurred. Baker stepped aside, and we resumed our walking. Two blocks up, we turned the corner at Alabama Avenue. Ahead lay City Hall, and a few blocks further south, the courthouse.

But this was as far as we could be allowed to go. Black-uniformed police fanned out across the street ahead of us, and Baker drove up, got out of his patrol car and announced our arrest.

Dr. King asked if we could pause for a prayer, and we all knelt on the cold, nubbly asphalt. Everything was going like clockwork.

VII

There were about 250 of us in the march, and it took hours to book us. The police herded us into the parking lot behind City Hall, and we stood there shivering in the cold, waiting our turn to go inside.

Eventually I was led in, fingerprinted and had a mug shot taken. Then I filed upstairs to the third floor, to what I now learned was the county jail. The city jail, too small to hold us all, was on the second floor.

Here the cells ran along two walls; above them, out of reach, was a row of small windows. Across from the cell block was a large day room, bare except for a couple of steel tables bolted to the floor, and a toilet in the corner. The marchers were crowded in the day room, and I moved in to join them.

There wasn't much for us to do but mill around, talk, and try to rest on the steel floor. We were all waiting for Dr. King to arrive, and tell us what to do next.

Finally, after what seemed hours, he and his right hand man, Ralph Abernathy, appeared. Later we found out that Wilson Baker had kept them till last, hoping they would decide not to be arrested after all. We greeted Dr. King with applause, expecting something like a resumption of the mass meetings at Brown Chapel.

But Dr. King was very subdued. He told us he was feeling hoarse, and would rather not preach. He suggested, instead, that we have "a Quaker-type meeting," in which people would speak simply "as the spirit moved," and he would listen along with the rest.

This was the first "Quaker-type meeting" I was ever part of, and it was like none of the thousand-plus Friends meetings I have attended since becoming involved with Quakers a year or so later.

It was, for one thing, much noisier. The spirit not only moved some of us to preach that afternoon; it also moved all of us to sing, several times, both freedom songs which I knew and gospel hymns which I didn't.

Being in jail added a special intensity to our voices and rhythmic accompaniment; the result was more than just music. Those of us pressed up against the walls soon found that if we slapped them in rhythm, they resounded like muffled calypso drums. When enough of us did it, the whole floor began to vibrate, as if the building itself was rocking and reverberating in time with us. And perhaps it was, because through the walls we soon heard an answering chorus from the other end of the third floor, where the women were being held. How I wish someone had recorded us!

Another intriguing feature of this meeting was that, notwithstanding Dr. King's invitation to anyone so moved to speak, the spirit nonetheless seemed to move rather directly and carefully down the local status hierarchy, until all the local dignitaries and preachers among us had had their say. Finally ordinary folks chimed in, and I even spoke up at one point, though I can't recall my message.

This meeting also went on longer than any "regular" Quaker meeting; two to three hours, it seemed. But finally, after one more heartfelt chorus of "We Shall Overcome," sung in muffled, echoed harmony with the women in their cell block, the meeting finally broke up, and we sank into a happy, exhausted disorder within the confines of our pen. Glancing up, I noticed that the windows above us had all been steamed over by our lusty exhalations.

As the group relaxed, Dr. King reverted to his pastoral role, and began moving along the edges of the day room, speaking through the bars to the regular county prisoners in their cells. Our coming had deprived them of access to the day room and the little chance to stretch that they had. Dr. King talked with each of them, listening sympathetically to their tales of woe and injustice, which carried a special poignancy on this afternoon.

He was still, I think, making these rounds when there was a clanging at the far end of the cell block, and the heavy barred door suddenly rolled back a few feet. We turned at the noise, and recognized Sheriff Clark's grim visage.

His eyes swept over the group, and then he began pointing and calling out: "You – King. Abernathy. Over here." He peered some more and pointed again, first at another staff worker. Then he pointed at me.

All at once I felt cold. It was safe in that crowded day room. Where were we going now? We had all heard stories of people who disappeared from southern jails, never to be seen again, unless to turn up floating in the river.

I moved reluctantly toward the door, aware of the suddenly sober expressions on the faces of the men I passed.

In the hallway the sheriff said gruffly, "Follow me." We did, down the stairs.

Emerging on the second floor, we were led to a cell in the city jail. In it were two sets of steel bunk beds, and another small window up high. The door rattled shut behind us, and Clark retreated into his own turf somewhere else in the building.

Then I understood. Clark was removing the "leadership" from the group upstairs, isolating the local men from the "professional agitators," in hopes of maintaining better control over the rest.

The realization made me smile. It was flattering to be included among those who threatened his status quo. But it was also a stretch. True, I was indeed a "professional," with paychecks to prove it; and certainly I was an outsider, but one still just beginning to find my way around in a bewildering new world. A "civil rights agitator"? Hardly.

Oh well. I took this implicit designation as a compliment. In any event, there in the cell I was as close as I had ever been to Dr. King, without dozens or hundreds of other people around as well. I began to hope there might be a chance to talk one-on-one, get to know him better, and maybe become better known to him as well.

Nothing like this happened immediately, however. Dr. King was not only hoarse, he was also bone tired, as he always was in those days. After some quiet huddling with Abernathy, he soon lay down on one of the bunks and dozed off.

I was too excited to follow his example, even though I'd

been up early and it was now late afternoon. The winter daylight was turning gray in the slit of the small high window. I noticed how quiet the cell was.

And then I also noticed the growling in my stomach. I hadn't eaten much breakfast, the march and waiting had taken hours, and no one had brought lunch to our shouting, singing crowd upstairs. In fact, I was starved. Would they bring us anything here?

VIII

After another hour or so, when the cell was dim in the dusk, there was a sudden noise in the hallway outside. A door banged, a light went on in the hallway, and metallic wheels squealed. A pungent aroma floated toward us as a voice called, "Dr. King! Oh, Dr. King! Ah got dinner for Dr. King!"

I turned to the cell door. Behind me Dr. King stirred.

A trusty appeared, a dark specter in kitchen whites, pushing a cart. "Dinner," he repeated. "Ah got dinner forCed cart and identified the aroma.

Collard greens. A single plate, piled with a mound of them, sat in the center of the cart. Were they steaming, or was it only my imagination?

I had never heard of, never mind eaten collard greens before coming to the South a few months earlier. But by now I knew them to be a humble southern vegetable, found in the more modest homes and establishments. Their odor was strong, the taste faintly bitter, though it mellowed somewhat after long simmering with chunks of fatback pork and salt. While collards were said to be very nutritious, I had not liked them much.

But now they looked succulent, and their fragrance set my mouth to watering.

The trusty had stopped, almost right in front of me. "Dr. King?" he called one more time, tentatively.

I heard motion from the bunks. Dr. King came past and reached through the bars to shake the trusty's hand. "How you doin'?" he asked, with a smile that was almost a grin, ready to make some small talk. "What you got there?"

I tuned out their quiet banter. My attention was drawn magnetically back to that steaming plate. As I gazed, it seemed to grow in size, til it looked as big as a platter, large enough to feed

all of us in the cell, with some left over.
But I knew this was illusion. It was merely a plate, and only one, and it was meant for Dr. King.
I reflected on this melancholy fact, then told myself sternly to buck up. The image of the army came back to mind: Dr. King was the general, I was the private. Armies win wars as much by the quality of their generalship as by the courage and luck of their grunts. Maybe more.
In our army there were 250 others like me upstairs, and many more than that outside, in the dark and edgy town. But there was only one of Dr. King, and even here he could still think, plan and give orders. It was, I considered, essential that he have a clear head, to calculate our next pivotal tactical and strategic moves. Thus it was quite proper that he maintain the energy and vigor needed to face whatever awaited him here in this jail, as well as the many hazards hovering beyond it.
So what if I was I hungry, even ravenous? I was young, relatively strong, temporarily out of action and in any case expendable. I could wait, while Dr. King did what was needed.
My gaze wandered back to the trusty. There I saw consternation was now woven into the creases of his weathered face, and began to listen again, as Dr. King said,
"– And that, my friend, is why I cannot eat your greens. I'm sorry."

IX

What?
I peered at Dr. King. Was he sick? Had I heard wrong? What had I missed? The trusty came to my rescue.
"Say what?" he murmured, as if he hadn't heard it either.
In reply, Dr. King began to explain.
The exact words are gone now, but the substance of what became a discourse is still as clear as if it were yesterday:
"You see," Dr. King began, "not long after I got involved in the move-ment [he always said the word as if it had three syllables: "move"– an unvocalized "ah"– "ment"], I had the opportunity, with the help of the Quakers, to visit India and study the work of Mahatma Gandhi, who had freed his country from British rule through campaigns of nonviolent resistance."
The trusty's face added a frown of incomprehension to the

furrows of confusion. I got the distinct impression he had no idea who Mahatma Gandhi was; for that matter, I barely did myself.

"And we found that Gandhi had gone to jail many times, sometimes spending long periods in prison with many of his followers. And after he had been in prison only a few times, Gandhi decided it was important to make the time count.

"So when he was in prison with a large number of people, he would organize them into a small representative democracy. 'We Indians say we want to be free and rule ourselves,' he told them. 'But if we are ever to make that happen, we need to learn and practice the tools of representative government.' So they held mock elections and practiced parliamentary procedure and all that."

I stole another look at the plate. Were the greens cooling? Did the trusty know what "parliamentary procedure" was?

"But that was not all," Dr. King went on. "Many Indians were illiterate, and so Gandhi asked those who could read to teach those who could not. And others who knew trades like carpentry, or professions like law and medicine, held classes to teach their fellows about practical skills and legal rights. Gandhi turned the British prisons into great schools of independence, right under the government's nose."

The trusty rubbed his chin and blinked. Was he, like me, wondering what any of this had to do with collard greens?

"Gandhi also worked to make the time in prison a unifying experience culturally," Dr. King explained. "In India there were two great religions, Hinduism and Islam, and the British schemed ceaselessly" [again the almost measured beats: "cease..less. . . ly"] "to sow discord and conflict between them, with much success.

"So Gandhi worked to heal these divisions, by holding religious services in prison every day. He used both Hindu scriptures and the Muslim Koran, showing respect and even reverence for these two ancient traditions. It worked too, while Gandhi was alive."

I glanced at Dr. King. There was a smile on his broad face; he had warmed to his subject.

"And not least," he said, "Gandhi decided that imprisonment was to be for him a time of religious retreat, with a regular routine of spiritual meditation and practice, to free and purify his spirit while he worked to free and purify his country."

Dr. King spread his hands out between the bars, gesturing

as if in a pulpit. "I was very moved by what I learned in India," he said, "and when Dr. Abernathy and I realized that we were likely to face arrest and jail repeatedly in our own struggle here, we agreed that we would follow Gandhi's example, to the extent that we were able."

Did this, I wonder, mean a literacy class in the morning? Or readings from the Koran? The trusty looked equally confused.

"Long ago," Dr. King resumed, and it sounded as if he was winding toward some kind of punch line, "Dr. Abernathy and I resolved that whenever we went to jail, we would try to be placed together, and together we too would make our prison sentences times of spiritual retreat and religious refreshment, with a regular routine of prayer, meditation and study."

Not to mention, I thought, some preaching now and again.

"And to put ourselves into the proper frame of mind for these times of retreat," Dr. King concluded, "we have always made it our practice that for the first two days we are in jail, we will fast."

X

So there it was, finally.

As I say, these were not his exact words, but the cadence and content are all there. In any case, when the trusty heard the word "fast," his mouth dropped open. Mine did, too.

The trusty frowned more deeply, and turned his head slightly, as if he was working up to ask a question, perhaps something like, "Say what?" Dr. King headed him off.

"And that, my friend, is why I very much appreciate the effort you've gone to," he said, "but I'm afraid I am unable to eat your greens."

"You mean – ?" croaked the trusty. Much of the rest of the disquisition may have gone over his head, but this last was sinking in.

Dr. King nodded.

The trusty looked genuinely confused."You mean,' he repeated, "you can't – ?"

Now Dr. King shook his head slowly.

The trusty looked at Abernathy, who had moved to Dr. King's elbow. He smiled apologetically, but shook his head also.

The trusty blinked and turned toward the other staffer, who

had hung back silently through this whole exchange. His head shook too.

The trusty stood there for a moment, without a clue as to what to do next.

And then, he looked at me.

XI

In the parable of the Good Samaritan, I have always thought the key to the story is in verse 33 of Luke's tenth chapter, where it says of the Samaritan who found the robbery victim, wounded and abandoned, that "his heart was moved with compassion."

I think I can say, with some humility, that when I saw the sense of loss and confusion on the trusty's face, my heart, like that of the Samaritan, was moved with compassion.

After all, it was easy to imagine what kind of life this man had, standing by the squeaky cart in the worn white uniform of a kitchen helper. We had heard similar laments from the county prisoners upstairs. I guessed he was probably a habitual drunk, petty thief, or some combination of the two. He probably had no job, like so many other black men around Selma, or couldn't keep one; perhaps he was among the many farm laborers who had been pushed out of the cotton fields by mechanization. Not dangerous, probably, except to himself or when drunk; otherwise, why would the police have let him work in the kitchen, where there must be knives and other potential weapons?

This was his bleak present, and probably his dreary future: helping prepare the Spartan prison fare for men, and perhaps a few women, slightly more wretched than himself, all wasting their lives in the obscure cells of a provincial city jail.

And then, like a breath of the divine, this day brought an astounding break in this routine: a flood of respectable citizens into the cellblocks; our thundering, rhythmic chorus of defiance and spirit which must have reverberated through these halls as well as our crowded warren upstairs. Even more amazing, from out of this inchoately marvelous mass, emerged the modern Moses, Dr. Martin Luther King, Jr., freshly back from Oslo and the Nobel Peace Prize, right into the hallways of his own tiny, godforsaken wasteland.

Why wouldn't he want to seize this moment of light, this

trembling interval of grace, and do something, do his best, for this apparition? I had heard about the anguished letters Dr. King received from black people across the country, people who thought he could work wonders, cure their diseases, or those of their suffering children, just by the laying on of his hands.

The trusty, though, had made no request, had asked for nothing. Rather, he had exercised his meager skill, and probably coaxed and begged his white keepers for leave, this once, this only once, to do for Moses the little he could do, bring to him a token of gratitude and honor, a sign of the exaltation that Dr. King, though all-too-human, had had laid on him for the benefit of us all, and especially for the least of them, of whom this trusty was a fitting embodiment.

He had made Dr. King a plate of greens. And now Dr. King had gently, but firmly, refused it.

What were homilies about someone named Gandhi compared to this?

How could I not be moved by this spectacle?

How could I not, in the face of it, make my own gesture, my own sacrifice?

I spoke:

"Um," I said, "you know, I'm really kind of new to this nonviolence business, and I never heard all this stuff about Gandhi before. So I – well, I haven't made any vows about fasting or praying or, um, anything like that."

The trusty blinked and listened to me bungle my sentences.

"So," I stumbled on, "what I mean is – I'd hate to see you go back to the kitchen , um, empty-handed, as it were."

I was losing him. "What I really mean is," I said, trying to get the lead out, "I mean, if it's all right with you, and Dr. King, well – I-I guess I'd be willing, um, willing to eat your greens."

The trusty blinked at me again. His gaze shifted questioningly to Dr. King. I followed, half afraid to look. But we both saw Dr. King give a slight nod and shrug, as if to affirm the innocence of my ignorance.

The trusty then looked at Abernathy, who nodded as well; the other civil rights worker followed.

Thus confirmed in the awareness that I was his fourth choice, I watched him slowly pick up the plate. He balanced it carefully, so as not to spill the collards' copious pot liquor, deftly opened the narrow slot in the door with the other hand, and slid it through. The plate was still warm in my hands. He passed me a plastic fork and knife.

I half-turned away from the others, all too conscious of their eyes on me. I was almost ready to cry out: oh god, forgive me! But the greens looked so good, the smell was intoxicating, irresistible.

I jabbed the fork into the heaped greens. But the tines sank only half an inch before sticking in something firmer, almost solid. What the –? Suspicion welled up. Could there be something sinister hidden in the chlorophyll? I scraped the greens to one side.

And there, beneath the facade of dull green, was not some toxin, nor another vegetable. Instead I found meat. Thick pink slices of fine country ham, a food of shameless luxury.

My mind raced as I cut and wolfed the chunks. This could not possibly be the everyday menu in this establishment; what cunning had he exercised to get them? The concealing arrangement of greens, which had seemed so random, suddenly took on an aspect almost of art.

What a dinner I had that night.

XII

Dr. King stayed in the Selma jail for several days. His term had rather little to do with segregationist repression. On the one hand, it was a coldly calculated matter of movement tactics, milking his arrest for as much publicity as was practical.

But it was also, after a fashion, Dr. King's way of cadging a favor from an unwilling host: courtesy of Wilson Baker, Dr. King had a few days of rest. His narrative for the trusty was not exaggerated; jail was a time of retreat, such as was virtually unknown and impossible in his life outside the bars.

As for me, I was bailed out late the following morning. For the privates in our forces, there were everyday matters to attend to; I had not earned any such respite. After all, as the army saying goes, rank hath its privileges.

XIII

Before I left, though, the time came when Dr. King did sit

and talk with me, man to man; and it was then that I missed my chance at a footnote in history. It happened this way:

After a month in the crash course atmosphere of Selma, I was full of earnest questions, about the movement and American society. Already I was wondering about the prospects and limits of reform.

"But Dr. King," I asked, "suppose we do overcome in Selma, and Negroes get the right to vote. Will that really make the changes America needs? Look at the North; many Negroes vote there, but I have heard you say yourself that in many ways they are no better off. How will voting end all the poverty and injustice here?"

Dr. King listened patiently to what could only be familiar, well-worn queries, and nodded. Yes, he replied, voting by itself will not be enough, though it is a tool we must fight for nonetheless. But–

– and here I approach an exact quote because the words still ring clear –

– if America is ever really to be redeemed, we will need to change the economic system. "We will have to adopt," he said it just this way, "a modified form of socialism."

Years later, when I read the fine biographies of Dr. King by scholars like David Garrow, I learned that Dr. King had been very careful, scrupulously careful, to avoid making such a statement in public, though the more searching scholars have turned up an unguarded allusion or two. And I understood why: the America he grew up in, besides its racism, was stalked by the forces of McCarthyism. Anti-Communist hysteria had claimed not a few of the most eminent black figures of his youth; Paul Robeson, W.E.B. DuBois, and others.

In the South, this witchhunt blended seamlessly with the crusade to preserve segregation. Even I had already seen a billboard bearing a picture of Dr. King at the integrated Highlander Folk Center in Tennessee, above the large, bold, and presumably damning caption: "Martin Luther King at Communist Training School."

Further, I learned from the biographies that one of Dr. King's closest white advisors, Stanley Levison, had indeed once been a Communist agent. Discovery of this connection had sent the FBI into fits, though it also appears Levison had abandoned the Kremlin by the time he became Dr. King's confidant.

Learning all this later, it became quite clear why Dr. King guarded his words in public on such matters. He was in the cross hairs in more ways than one. And this knowledge likewise makes it clear–achingly, utterly obvious, what my next question to him ought to have been. Namely,

"*Dr. King, what do you mean by 'a modified form of socialism?'*"

After all, we have seen that "socialism" comes in numerous forms. Indeed, according to many conservatives, a "modified form of socialism" is just what the United states has had, certainly since the New Deal years of Franklin Roosevelt. What, amid the plethora of forms and definitions, was Dr. King actually talking about?

I can offer a speculation, based on all I have learned about him: He was not any kind of orthodox Marxist. I think he was talking about something like the mixed economies of Scandinavia which seemed so successful in those years, where the state owned much, but by no means all of the productive enterprise, and was heavily present even in the private sector. What some have called "social democracy," sidling away from the hazardous associations of the other S-word.

That is what I *think*. And if I had confirmed this by drawing him out, I would have chiseled a permanent niche for myself, small but significant, in the annals of Dr. King's life and thought.

But I don't know for sure, because instead of asking, "Dr. King, what do you mean by a 'modified form of socialism?'" I merely nodded knowingly, as if I understood him perfectly.

The moment passed. The bailiff's keys soon jangled in the door, and then I was out, on the street, headed for Brown Chapel and a return to work. I took many precious things away from that brief sojourn; but one of them was not, alas, a footnote in history.

Chapter Two
Night March

I

Fast forward two weeks. I had been arrested again on February third, marching outside the courthouse, and spent the following ten days in jail. Half that time I was back in the county's dayroom on the third floor of City Hall, with a dozen or so teenagers. Then our smaller band was bussed out to a state-run prison camp outside of town, where we joined other new arrestees, and slept on a concrete floor of an unheated dormitory. That sojourn has many stories of its own, which will be told in due course.

While I was inside, the tense, three-cornered jockeying among Dr. King, Wilson Baker and Sheriff Clark intensified, with the attention of the mass media as the immediate prize. The list of players was also expanding: Governor George Wallace became increasingly vocal in his opposition to the movement, and his state troopers, under their notoriously segregationist commander, Col. Al Lingo, were more and more visible in the area.

To us, the troopers were a truly ominous sight: their large blue and grey Fords featured confederate battle flag license plates, and the message they conveyed seemed all too obvious. Also obvious, but unspoken, was the fact that Wilson Baker was as anxious to keep them out of town as we were.

This struggle seesawed back and forth irresolutely until just after I was released. Then, on Tuesday, February 17, it took a decisive turn.

That morning a small group of marchers went to the courthouse, led by Rev. C.T. Vivian. C.T., as we called him, was wiry and good-natured, but also fearless and one of King's more sharp-tongued colleagues. It was raining, but when Sheriff Clark saw the group coming, he locked the courthouse doors and left the marchers standing in the drizzle.

Sensing an opportunity, Vivian mounted the courthouse steps and began preaching angrily at Clark, until the sheriff finally lost his cool and unlocked the door long enough to reach out and deck Vivian with one solid roundhouse punch. Clark then arrested Vivian and dragged him away, bleeding but still protesting loudly and eloquently.

The whole shocking scene had been caught by television cameras from across the street. It seemed to call for some response, and it came at that evening's mass meeting in Brown Chapel, when Dr. King announced that he was preparing to call for night marches.

Night marches were especially dangerous. In the summer of 1964, King and others of his staff had led numerous night marches St. Augustine, Florida, where the local sheriff was known to be in close collusion with the Ku Klux Klan. More than one of these marches had been attacked by whites, and I had heard these marches referred to by older civil rights workers to as the very archetypes of terror. "Man, after those marches I was *glad* to get inside a nice, safe jail," one veteran told me.

I believed it. The cover of darkness had been a standard weapon of the Klan and other southern vigilantes. But this very fact increased the tactical value of a night march. It was also, Dr. King, rightly guessed, the right moment for such a march in Alabama. If it scared us, it would also scare the authorities, or at least Baker. And it would likewise bring the press back in droves.

II

Dr. King was as good as his word. The very next night, from the nearby town of Marion, a march set out from a small black church on a corner of the town square. C.T. Vivian, just out of jail, was in the lead.

The response was swift and violent: The street lights suddenly went out, and the marchers were attacked by state troopers and others. A well-known reporter for NBC TV, Richard Valeriani, was beaten bloody; and a young local man named Jimmie Lee Jackson was shot by a trooper. Jim Clark was spotted on the scene, in civilian clothes, carrying a nightstick.

After Marion, events moved swiftly: squads of state trooper cars pulled into Selma, with the courthouse as their stronghold. On Saturday, February 20, Governor Wallace issued a proclamation banning night marches. Dr. King spent the weekend in bed with the flu, but returned to Selma on Monday, to visit Jimmie Lee Jackson in the hospital, lead a march to the heavily patrolled courthouse, and then speak to a packed mass meeting that night.

The mass meeting was already noisily underway when I arrived at Brown Chapel that night. I came ready to do my part, which I presumed would be the usual, marching close to Dr. king as one of his shields. From the volume and timbre of the singing and clapping, I could tell that the people were especially enthusiastic. They were ready to march, to follow Dr. King anywhere.

III

That is, most of them were.

Beyond the spotlight glare of his fame, Dr. King had his detractors within the ranks, and this was true in Selma as elsewhere. The most vocal critics were found among the staff of SNCC, the Student Nonviolent Coordinating Committee. As a newcomer, I puzzled over their complaints, trying to make out not only the specifics, but also their emotional substrate–not just the words, but the music.

SNCC represented a younger, mostly secular, and more militant generation of activists, many of whom were quite cynical about the black clergy which Dr. King represented, and the Christianity from which he drew his rhetoric. They also resented the media's overwhelming focus on Dr. King as the personification of the civil rights struggle.

But it also seemed that many of them disliked King personally. Their brief against him included a number of points:

He was a publicity hound, they charged, always staying close to the TV cameras, and seldom lingering in a place after they had left.

He exploited local campaigns for the publicity and financial benefit of his organization, SCLC, leaving local leadership at higher risk of white backlash and reprisal after he left town, and less able to cope with it.

And not least, it was often hinted that he was a physical coward, who carefully avoided the really hazardous marches, leaving them to underlings while he hobnobbed with senators and millionaires, collecting awards and fat speaking fees.

Besides the general complaints, there was a specific history to this antagonism in Selma: SNCC workers had done the original organizing here, three years before King came, and they had taken more than their share of licks for it from Clark and his posse, with little to show for it but their scars. Some felt Dr. King and SCLC were now moving in on their turf and taking credit for all their hard work and suffering.

Leading a night march, besides its publicity value, was an ideal way to banish such charges. And there was certainly no sense of doubt or skepticism in the crowd. They were ready to hit the street; anxious, even.

IV

I lingered for awhile in the back of the church, joining in with the singing, and enjoying the fervent preaching. Dr. King was not on the platform yet, but I was sure he would be there shortly. Anyway, by this time I knew that some of his lieutenants, such as Ralph Abernathy and James Bevel, when at their best were even more moving and powerful in the pulpit than Dr. King. I was happy to listen to them, and gain strength from the group.

But after two, three rousing sermons and more freedom songs, something about the mass meeting began to feel out of rhythm. Dr. King still hadn't taken his seat on the platform; the sermons were being given by second-tier staff, along with a couple of alumni from out of town, and their fervent homilies were taking longer than usual.

They're pushing it, I suddenly realized. They're stretching out their material, straining and pumping up the rhetoric like balloons. They're *stalling*.

What was going on? Dr. King was often late, but I was pretty sure he and his inner circle were all in town. Where were they? Something was up. What was it?

I decided to find out. Making my way up a side aisle, I went through a door and down a short hall behind the platform, to where there was a kitchen and a couple of small offices.

The singing and preaching were muffled now, and voices came from one of the offices. Opening the door, I saw several of the staff gathered around a desk, with others behind them. Among them were the real insiders: Ralph Abernathy, Andy Young, Hosea

Williams, James Bevel. I slipped in and stood at the back, listening. Andy Young was talking into a black telephone receiver. I sensed he had been talking for awhile. Then he handed it to Dr. King.

"Yes, Mr. Marshall," Dr. King said into it. "Good of you to call."

Then he listened, murmuring occasional monosyllabic responses.

"Who is it?" I whispered to someone. "What's going on?"

"Burke Marshall," came the quiet reply.

I knew the name. Burke Marshall was Deputy United States Attorney General for Civil Rights. He was probably calling from Washington.

"I understand your concern, sir," Dr. King said after an interval. He was speaking slowly and deliberately. "I realize that it's dangerous. But as you can understand, we live with danger all the time. And as I have said to the people here, I'm going to march tonight, and that's what I expect to do." His voice was calm and sounded tired.

The night march. A call from Burke Marshall. I was recalling St. Augustine and putting two and two together when Dr. King thanked Marshall again, said goodbye, and hung up.

"He says there's a group of Klansmen in the area who are looking for trouble," Dr. King reported. "He doesn't have enough federal marshals to protect us, and he wants us to call off the march."

Scanning the rest of the group, I could tell they had already heard the gist of this message. Somebody, maybe one of the SNCC staff, jeered quietly. "Hell, if we called off every march where there was danger we'd never march at all."

Some others nodded at this, and maybe – my memory is not clear – Dr. King smiled wanly. But the mood was clearly subdued. The noise of singing and clapping from the church swelled and rumbled through the wall.

Dr. King stirred in his chair. "Well, Andy," he said, "I guess we'd better go on out there and get ready."

But the phone rang again before he could rise. Someone else, probably Andy, picked it up, spoke quietly into it, and listened for a few moments. Then he put his hand over the mouthpiece and spoke to Dr. King.

"It's Katzenbach. For you."

V

Nicholas Katzenbach; I knew that name also. The Attorney General of the United States, point man on civil rights for the President, doubtless calling from his big office in the sprawling, granite Justice Department building in Washington.

Dr. King took the phone, said hello, and listened patiently in his turn. Then he repeated what he had just said to Burke Marshall: "I appreciate your concern, sir," he concluded. "But as I have said, our plan is to march, and we're going to do that. We can't let threats of violence deter us. I understand sir." There was some more monosyllabic dialogue. Then "Thank you very much."

He hung up again. As he had listened, and then talked, I felt the room getting somehow quieter, even with the crowd's exuberance echoing around it. I also felt colder. Glancing from side to side, I saw that the faces of all the insiders, Andy, Hosea, Abernathy, were very long and somber. Their eyes had widened, just a little, but enough to notice. And despite the sense of chill, there was sweat on some foreheads.

They were afraid, I realized. But not they, *we*. I was becoming afraid also.

Andy and Dr. King were repeating for the rest of us what they had heard:

Katzenbach had underlined Burke Marshall's report. There was a Klan hit team in the area, and they were planning to make their assault in two groups. The Carver Homes, which surrounded the church, were built in neat parallel rows at right angles to Sylvan Street, and were well-suited for the Klan's purpose, especially at night. The only illumination was a few porch lights.

"They'll wait til the march gets most of the way down the block," Andy explained. "Then one group will come between the houses right across from the church with billy clubs and who knows what else, and jump the march there."

But the first charge would be only a tactical diversion. As everyone's attention shifted to the melee that would follow, marchers would begin to scatter. In the confusion, another team would steal down between houses closer to the corner, aiming for their real target – the front of the column, and Dr. King.

As I took in this explanation, and visualized the impending scene, time seemed to slow down, and the whole room took on a certain unreal, almost dreamlike quality.

A moment of – what, truth? – was upon us. We had a threat of imminent violence, delivered not by some anonymous postcard or a heavy-breathing phone call, but by the two highest law enforcement officials of the U.S. government.

"Katzenbach said they don't have enough marshals in the area to protect the march, and they can't count on the sheriff or the police."

"Count on them?" someone scoffed. "Hell, that posse *is* the Klan."

My knees began to tremble, just a little. I glanced down nervously, hoping the motion wasn't visible through my overalls. Where would I be when the march left the church? Probably where I had been on those previous occasions, marching near Dr. King with the others. Being a sitting duck, or rather a walking one.

My bladder begin to make itself felt. I had read about this in soldiers facing battle. Well, I was a soldier, if a nonviolent one, and would follow orders, however shakily. Just please, God, don't let me pee my pants.

VI

There was more talk, a jumbled mixture of bravado and barely-concealed apprehension; the words are lost to me now. But as they swirled anxiously around us, I slowly became aware of silence at their center: Dr. King behind the desk, listening but not quite seeming to hear. By now, a sense of terror at the attack to come was palpable among us. All of us, that is, except Dr. King.

Then it was apparent to me that he was somehow disconnected from the rest of us, or at least, disconnected from our fear. There he was, only a few feet away, listening and talking quietly; I heard him clearly despite the din of the mass meeting.

And yet it was also as if he was floating far above us, on a raft of complete calm atop the swirling current of our dread.

One by one the members of his inner circle began raising objections, suggesting that the march could in fact be put off. They didn't actually admit to their fear, but the fact of it was evident, and I was glad to hear them speak up.

Dr. King remained calm, immoveable. "We've got to march," he repeated, adding that it was time to go speak to the people, to reinforce their nonviolent discipline in the face of provocation, and then to march.

As this parley continued, I saw clearly something else I hadn't seen before: the falsity of the rumors of Dr. King's cowardice in the face of physical danger. They were not just false, but laughably so.

Everyone in that room, including me, was terrified, and with good reason.

Everyone, that is, except Dr. King. He was a rock. Standing at the rear of the room, my fear soon mingled with a kind of awe at the utter fearlessness he was manifesting. This sense of awe deepened as the moments passed.

VII

Much later, after he was dead and I had learned more about him, I gained a certain perspective on this moment. He had, after all, faced violence before: in September, 1958 he had been stabbed by an unbalanced woman at a bookstore in Harlem. The seven-inch blade sank into his chest very near his heart, and he had to sit motionless until help came, to prevent it from slicing the aorta and killing him.

His house in Montgomery had been bombed. A neo-Nazi had attacked him in Selma just a few weeks earlier.

Among the death threats which came to him almost daily, more than a few had been real and credible.

But there was more. In November, 1963, after watching the funeral cortege of John F. Kennedy, King suddenly turned to his wife Coretta and said, with a sober matter-of-factness, "That is what will happen to me."

VIII

So he knew. By February of 1965, he had known for a long time, and evidently accepted, that for him, it was not a question of whether violent death would come, but only a matter of when and where.

This knowledge makes more intelligible the memory of that moment in the back of Brown Chapel AME Church. The rest of us in that room did not know what kind of death awaited us; Dr. King evidently did, and by whatever process, was at peace with it. If that end was to arrive this night, then so be it.

It was Andy Young, one of the shrewdest of his aides and

a veteran of the St. Augustine attacks, who finally found the argument which could deflect this irresistible force, could budge this immovable object. He spoke over the voices of the crowd swelling into another round of the song, "You Got to Do What the Spirit Say Do," with its verse: "If the Spirit Say March, You Got to March, Oh Lord. . . ."

"Martin," he said, "I know we're ready to march" – by which he really meant, *you* are ready – "but what about the people out there?"

They didn't have the benefit of these phone calls from Washington, he went on. They didn't know how imminent the risks really were that night. It was one thing for us, in this room, to go out there. That was our job, and we knew what we were getting into. But the people?

Of course, they had been told it was risky. And they already knew well enough the hazards of being assertive Negroes in the Deep South. And yet, how many of them would still want to march if they knew what we know – if they had sat through these phone calls?

As he spoke, I saw that this plea, for it was nothing else, was sinking in. Again, much later I understood better that Dr. King, beneath the layers of celebrity that had been congealing around him for a decade, was at heart a pastor, a shepherd of souls. I had glimpsed this in his quiet talks with the prisoners in the county jail. And that's how he had started out in Montgomery; if fate had not intervened, that is where he would likely have been in 1965, preparing to succeed to his father's pulpit at Ebenezer Baptist Church in Atlanta.

In the gospels, Jesus declares that it is the shepherd's role to lay down his life for his flock. But was it right to lay down the lives of the flock for the shepherd? This was the burden of Andy's argument, and I could see he was scoring points.

Dr. King began to nod. "Maybe you're right, Andy," he said at length. "It is a different thing for them than for us." If he didn't intend the "us" ironically, I certainly heard it thus. "I suppose we'd better put off the march for a day or so."

There was a collective sigh of relief from the rest of the room. The trembling in my knees began to subside; my bladder seemed less urgently full. There were a few barks of nervous laughter.

With this decision made, the talk quickly turned technical,

about who would call Washington back with the news, and how to maintain the interest of the media for another week or so.

But this minutiae was drowned out by the crescendo of another song: "Ain't Gonna Let Nobody Turn Me Round. . ."

"Well," Dr. King said calmly, "I guess we'd better go out there and tell them."

IX

That was when I abruptly grasped another critical dimension of this scene: When Dr. King went out to the platform, quieted the cheers, and then told the frenzied crowd that plans had changed, that they were to put a lid on their enthusiasm and go quietly home, he wasn't going to tell them that it was to foil a Klan hit squad poised outside for the kill.

Instead, he would say something eloquently vague about the importance of seeing and responding to kairotic moments – he liked this New Testament term for God's timing, even though, or perhaps just because, few of his hearers would know what it meant.

But among the audience there would also be the skeptics, the mockers. They would not be fooled by talk of kairos. They would hear about the phone calls from Washington, and they would say, "You see? He chickened out. The Klan came around, and he ran away."

I knew that's what would be said, and soon enough it was. But I also knew – I had seen, in a way I could almost touch – that this claim too was completely mistaken.

Dr. King was not afraid of the Klan and their hit squads. And there is more: when it meant the safety of his flock, he was not even afraid of looking like he was afraid, as he stood on the platform that night and said a benediction on the wilting, frustrated and confused crowd that had waited for him so long and so passionately.

Coming home that night, I could not tell which had been the more intense, exhausting experience: what had happened to me personally in that back room, or what I had seen in Dr. King. Since then, the balance has become much more clear: my fears were ordinary, familiar and appropriate, nothing to be ashamed of. But what was made manifest through Dr. King that night was something else again. I have never seen anything like it, before or since.

Reader Advisory

In my experience, there were three concentric circles of people around Dr. King, distinguishable by the names they used.

First, and innermost, were people close enough to him to address him as "Martin." There were not many of these.

Then there was a second, larger circle, people of his acquaintance, who spoke of him as "Martin," not to his face, but in the hearing of other people, to convey the impression that they were in the first circle.

And finally there was everyone else, to whom he was simply Dr. King.

I am, and always was, in this third circle. Yes, I was "on his staff." Yes, he knew my name, especially after our night in jail. But I never flattered myself that I was "close" to him. The military analogy still holds: he was the general, I was a private.

The previous chapters offered my best Dr. King stories. I put them first, admittedly, to draw you into the narrative.

But now the focus shifts. This is, after all, a memoir, about my experience in Selma, leading up to, during and after the voting rights campaign there. And for most of it, Dr. King recedes into the background – a continuing presence, but not at center stage.

I hope you'll want to read the rest of this story anyway.

Chapter Three
Nudges

I

Let's take a step back. Who was I, and how did I come to be in Selma that February?

Good questions, made more pointed because I didn't fit the profile of the 1960s white civil rights activist. I wasn't a red diaper baby; my parents were outwardly apolitical, my father a career Air Force officer.

I had never been to a folk festival, and had barely heard of Woody Guthrie or Leadbelly. I wasn't raised Jewish, Quaker or Unitarian, but Catholic, of a distinctly conservative Irish sort. In 1960, my freshman year at Colorado State University, it's not clear whether I even knew what a labor union was, and that fall I thought I preferred Richard Nixon for President over John Kennedy.

No question, I was notably insular and uninformed. In fact, I was almost entirely oblivious to the famous milestones of the early sixties civil rights resurgence, though approaching twenty and regarded as a bright student.

Lunch counter sit-ins? Freedom Rides?
I'm afraid I don't recall, your honor.
James Meredith? Mississippi burning?
Umm, vaguely.
Birmingham–fire hoses, dogs, and Bull Connor?
Nope.

If there had been an entrance exam for the movement, I would have failed it miserably.

Ransacking my childhood memories, only two items bob to the surface from the murky depths as possible precursors.

One is environmental: I was an Air Force brat. In the 1950s the Air Force, like the rest of the military, was officially desegregated, and had been since Harry Truman gave orders to this effect. To be sure, the reality of service life fell considerably short of this standard. I had no black friends as a child; we had, as I recall, exactly one black student in my Air Force high school.

But what this might mean came to light one hot day in 1956. My father was driving from Travis Air Force Base near San Fran-cisco to a base in Louisiana, where we were to climb on a plane for Ramey Air Force Base in Puerto Rico. When he stopped at a dusty crossroads gas station in Texas, I made a beeline for the bathroom.

Turning the corner of the station, I saw not one, but two doors marked "Men," one for "White" and the other for "Colored."

I could not have said why, but this pairing struck me like a slap. I glanced inside both: the Colored toilet was smaller, darker, and uncleaned. I went in there anyway, defiantly, and returned to the car feeling shaky and out of breath. It is my only memory of that long drive.

This was a vivid incident, certainly, but also a brief and isolated one. Are these enough to have predicted my arrival in the movement eight years later? I don't think so.

So how did I end up in the thick of it?

Perhaps it's a conceit of middle age, but I prefer to mull over this last question in another, a theological form:

Is there such a force as Providence? Can I look back over my life and identify little jogs and nudges to my personal history, coincidences that directed it this way and that, in a pattern that has some larger, perhaps transcendently-directed meaning?

Thus grandly phrased, such a query is of course humanly unanswerable, and pretentious to boot. Doesn't every event affect every other anyway, in an impossibly complicated web of ramifications, a near cosmic ebb and flow?

Sure. But I ask the question that way all the same; I'm a theological sort. I was then, in my callow way.

Besides, when I look back, it seems as if I can perceive such "nudges," even while admitting the overall pattern they might be outlining is as yet obscure.

Acknowledging the intractability of the question, it's still clear to me that if there is such a thing as Providence, it left two fat thumbprints on my course in the early fall of 1963.

The first came in the form of a certified letter which arrived at my fraternity house in Fort Collins, Colorado.

II

My senior year at CSU was just underway. What ideas I had about life and work after graduation were hazy to say the least, and consisted mainly of negatives, things I was not going to do. Some of these, such as not going to work for a big corporation, I could have written down; others, were discovered only when they could not be ignored any longer.

The letter cut through my denial about one of the latter items. It was from the campus Air Force ROTC, and carried a summons which can be fairly summarized as: "Fager, get your butt over here, this Friday, without fail." It was signed by Major Calvin G. Bass.

I don't think I'd ever received a certified letter before, so the missive had its intended effect. That Friday, I duly presented myself in Major Bass's office in the small ROTC building on the south side of the campus.

Major Bass wanted to be his usual affable, concerned self, but felt obliged to take on a stern demeanor for me, which didn't actually fit him very well. Trained as a combat pilot in 1944 and 1945, he was just heading for the Pacific when Japan surrendered.

Major Bass had stayed in the Air Force and kept flying, but now he had been a bomber pilot for twenty years without ever having dropped a bomb. A cherubic fellow, slightly plump and scholarly, he was finishing a Ph.D. in history; he hardly looked the part of a nuclear warrior. Maybe that was why he was teaching ROTC instead of commanding a bomber squadron somewhere.

Major Bass's life, what I knew of it, displayed some of the same themes as that of my own father: Because Callistus Fager had been a few years older when he came off a small Kansas farm for pilot training, there was still plenty of World War II left for him. He flew bombers over North Africa and Europe, managing to put in the required forty missions without a scratch, though with many close calls. Like many other veterans, he didn't talk about his war experiences much. And like Major Bass, he stayed in the Air Force, putting in thousands more flying hours, but like my instructor, never again dropping a bomb in combat.

As a result, I was raised on Air Force bases, the last of which was Francis E. Warren AFB in Cheyenne, Wyoming. The oldest of what ultimately totaled eleven children, the military was all I knew about, and as I went from high school to college, I gravitated reflexively toward it. First I applied to the Air Force Academy and almost gained entry; then I enrolled at Colorado State, where ROTC was required for freshman and sophomore males. For a long time it had seemed I was on track to follow in the footsteps of both men: my father, and the would-be mentor before me now.

But in September of 1963, all that was about to change.

"Okay, Chuck," Major Bass said as sternly as he could, "why don't you tell me what the hell is going on?"

III

The truth was, a lot had been going on.

Major Bass liked me; I knew that. I was even something of a protégé, whom he had been grooming and guiding toward a bright future in the service. In turn, I appreciated the attention and respected him. But somewhere, just below the surface of consciousness, I guess I had long known a morning meeting like this one was coming.

In my first year at CSU, playing off my background in an Air Force family, plus a near-miss at the Air Force Academy, I had won the medal as Outstanding Freshman Cadet. The next year I was Commander of the Sabres, our drill team, and even won a trophy or two.

Then came my junior year. Something came unstuck then, but I'm not sure what. The summer before, I did travel to New York, to work as a counselor in an affluent Jewish summer camp, where I broke personal precedent and proved very appealing to some of the female counselors. Maybe my first glimpse of the Big Apple, exposure to a challenging new culture, and the whiff of *la dolce vita* stirred something.

But besides a bit of travel, there had also been two other themes developing for me: one was writing, and the other was religion.

Religion was the odder of the two, because my relation to it was strictly one of a rebel and insurgent. I had thrown off what I saw as the shackles of Catholicism in high school; in college Carl Jung seemed to make the most sense of religion for me: he took it seriously, as an authentic phenomenon, not just a disguise for sex or aggression as did Freud. But Jung was not confined to any of what he called "the creeds," he saw the telltale footsteps of the ineffable in many religions.

I didn't know where that was going; but I took as many religious courses as CSU had to offer.

As for the other theme, I could trace it back to the second day of tenth grade, at Ramey Air Force Base in Puerto Rico. We had a new English teacher at the high school that year, a Mr. Brown. On the first day, to get acquainted with us and our skills, he told us to compose an essay on the spot, on an assigned topic.

I have no idea now what mine was about. But the next day when the bell rang, Mr. Brown, who had a flair for the dramatic, walked into the classroom, carrying our papers, and stopped in front of my desk. He paused for a moment, to be sure the entire class was paying attention, then dropped my theme on the desk, and announced loudly:

"Fager, you have a future in writing."

And so, more or less, it had turned out. By the fall of 1963, I had been editor of the CSU yearbook and the literary magazine, and was now about to begin producing a weekly column for the campus paper, *The Collegian*. Where any of this might lead, I had no idea, no plan, not a clue.

But one evident outcome of these factors, combined with the bit of travel and who knows what else, was that by my junior year ROTC was no longer fun. I became rather a goof-off, skipping class and dozing through the sessions I did attend. Accordingly, my grade sank from the expected, almost automatic A to an abysmal, practically unheard of C in my first term.

Major Bass, who had previously watched my progress with benign, encouraging interest, became quietly alarmed. He clearly wanted to buck me up, and get me back on track toward a good record and that second lieutenant's commission.

Sometime in the early spring of 1963 he made his move.

IV

"Chuck," he asked one day, "how'd you like to go for a ride in a jet?"

He had scheduled us for a private test drive in a T-38, a jet trainer from Lowry Air Force Base in Denver. Clearly he figured that a spin in this modern plane, which would loom large when I went on from ROTC to active duty and pilot training, would remind me of what was in store and renew my enthusiasm.

We drove to Denver, put on green flight suits and helmets, then climbed in, lowered the cockpit canopy and took off. Major Bass climbed smoothly and headed us south, along the front range of the Rockies, a patchwork landscape of dead grass, tan and craggy mountain grey, streaked with the white of receding snow banks.

I was in the back, bemusedly watching it all go by. The sky was clear, and the sun beat down on me through the plexiglass. We soon were near Colorado Springs, and passed over the shiny aluminum triangles of the new chapel at the Air Force Academy, my almost alma mater, then banked and turned north, back toward Denver.

My earphones buzzed, and Major Bass spoke.

"You know, Chuck," he said, "when I'm up here like this, I can't think of anything else I'd rather do than fly." The tinny intercom did not diminish the fervor in his voice.

But I recoiled from the words, almost as from an electric shock. If I answered at all, it was only a noncommittal murmur.

That's because when he spoke, I had instantly realized that there were half a dozen things I could think of that I'd rather be doing than flying: pursuing one of my ill-fated romances; writing for the campus paper; reading about any one of several literary-historical subjects; listening to classical music; even hanging out in the library.

I faked gratitude for Major bass's generous gesture, but the prospect of an Air Force career for me, following in either his or my father's footsteps, probably ended on that flight.

V

The next summer, between junior and senior years, a month's tour in ROTC summer camp was required; I was sent to a base in Salina, Kansas. There we were up by dawn, marching to meals and everywhere else under a broiling sun that pushed temperatures above one hundred degrees almost every day. I was constantly tired and hated every minute of it.

Well, almost every minute. There were two highlights to our month, which offered clear portents of my straying from the old, presumptive path toward something new:

The first was a long trip in a big KC-135 jet tanker, which took us from Kansas to North Dakota and back. We were told that somewhere over North Dakota the plane would link up with and refuel a B-52 bomber in mid-air, and we could watch this coupling through special viewing ports. The other cadets were excited; this was going to be fun.

I was looking forward to the trip too, but with a different agenda. Having watched many Air Force movies, including hours of propaganda documentaries, I had seen the refueling process a dozen times on screen. I was after something different: almost as soon as we were airborne and out of our seat belts, I scouted the cabin until I found what I was seeking: a nylon bunk folded against the fuselage wall.

Collaring a crewman, I asked innocently, "How does this work?"

He obligingly showed me, pulling it down and snapping it into place.

"Hey, that's neat," I said. "Let me try it out."

I hopped up, lay down, and was soon blissfully asleep. A cadet shook me when the refueling was about to happen, but I waved him away with a curse, and slept until it was time to land. Few of my comrades believed it when I insisted that I had enjoyed the trip as much as anyone, but it was true.

The other big event was a three-day stint to be spent hanging out in the base facility where we were likely to work once we were commissioned. Until now, I had been on a pilot's track, and the camp commander automatically signed me up to spend several days in the flight hangars.

As soon as the list was posted, I went to the commander and asked for a change: "Let me go to the PIO," I pleaded.

He looked at me as if I was daft. The Public Information Office was where the base newspaper was produced. The list of cadets interested in it was rather shorter than that for other locations; in fact, there was no one on it at all. But I insisted, and the choice was mine, so the commander shrugged and put my name down.

When the day came I showed up at the PIO, to the amazement of two bored lieutenants who were putting in their time there. They spent an hour or so telling me about pampering VIPS and fielding questions from local reporters when some airman smashed up a car. Then they ran out of things to talk about.

I was ready to fill the gap. "I'd like to go over to the base library," I told them, "and do some research on this."

They shrugged; sure, what the hell?

I had already scoped out the library's location. And I also knew that, beginning in the late fifties, the Air Force had decided to spend a bundle upgrading base libraries, to make them conducive to self-improvement by the ranks. Soon I was comfortably ensconced there, reading a novel, writing long letters to my girlfriend, and listening to classical music, all in air-conditioned comfort. I spent the rest of our on-the-job tour very agreeably there.

VI

After my camp experience, I should have known what was coming; but denial is a powerful force. Returning to CSU, I was advised that there were ROTC meetings for seniors to attend, to get the program organized for the term. Despite my crummy performance the year before, my name turned up slotted in the number four position in the senior cadet corps. I could sense Major Bass's influence in this positioning: a new cadet commander was selected for each of the year's three quarters, and the title would look very good on your record. If my performance turned around in the fall term, I had a real shot at being commander in the winter or spring.

But it was not to be. Several senior meetings were scheduled; I "forgot" and skipped them all. It was this absenteeism which finally produced the certified letter's summons. And then, there in his office, Major Bass's puzzled, irritated inquiry: "Chuck, why don't you tell me what the hell is going on?"

Squirming in my chair, I realized that nothing but an honest answer would do. I owed Major Bass that much.

But what was an honest answer? I had avoided thinking about ROTC since camp ended.

Major Bass's gaze was steady. "Well?"

After another moment of hesitation, I blurted out a truth I hadn't actually acknowledged until that very moment: "Sir, I just can't do it any more."

VIII

Major Bass did not give up easily. His gravity quickly shifted to an effort to cajole me back onto the reservation. He told me he understood I was more interested in things like English and writing than I was in flying. Well, the Air Force needed English teachers and writers too. In fact, he knew faculty people at the Air Force Academy, and they were looking for good people in those departments.

For that matter, he went on, warming to the topic, the service would send me to the best graduate school I could get into, pay all my tuition and expenses, and throw in a lieutenant's salary besides. Then, with a master's or a doctorate in the bag, he was sure I'd be a shoo-in at the Academy, teaching the Air Force's best and brightest.

He was smiling by now. This was a hell of a deal he was offering.

Of course, he added, there was a price tag: for every year that the Air Force financed my graduate education, a year onto would be added to my four-year obligation to serve. I knew this already.

But this was no big deal, he said. He grinned at me and opened his hands in a no-sweat gesture:

"Heck, Chuck," he said, "you only pay for it in years of your life."

For the second time, his words hit me like a physical blow. This sentence resounds in memory as thunderously now as it did more than forty-five years ago.

"Years of my life?" My eyes widened. I thought, I screamed internally: *"Years of my life? That's all I've got."*

I must have stared at him. I didn't answer right away, but the churning in my stomach, made plain that I couldn't say yes. Major Bass saw my hesitation; did he also see the panic?

"You don't have to answer right now," he soothed. "It's Friday. Think about it over the weekend, and come back and see me on Monday."

I rose, trembling with relief at the reprieve.

"But Chuck," he warned, "Monday is the deadline. I've got to know for sure by then."

I promised he would.

IX

    I didn't really spend much time agonizing over the next two days. Once obliged to actually think about it, it was obvious that ROTC was not for me. Not anymore. But over that weekend my resolve firmed up, and by Monday morning, I was able to tell Major Bass my decision calmly and forthrightly.
    He was disappointed, but he had clearly seen it coming. And when I finished, he sent me upstairs to see his boss, Colonel Bexfield, the PMST, Professor of Military Science and Tactics.
    I knew Colonel Bexfield, because the year before I had taken an honors seminar with him. Even then, it was unusual for ROTC to make it into the select honors curriculum; it was considered very soft, even slightly silly as an academic subject.
    Sure enough, the seminar was an easy grade. But the subject, a study of military interventions, has proved more durable than I ever expected. The Colonel defined "intervention" as military action by one country against another without a formal declaration of war. He explained that nations (especially big ones) "intervene" thus in other nations (especially smaller ones) when:
    A. They want something the other country has;
    B. They think they can take it by force;
    C. Their claim is not recognized by other nations; but
    D. They think they can get away with it anyway.
    An easy grade, yes; but hardly a joke. Within two years, the colonel's insights were being reflected back at me in the headlines of every American newspaper, and they still make sense of much of what has happened in the world ever since.
    The colonel remembered our course, and was both pleased and sorry to see me. He interrogated me gently, and I told him what I had told major Bass: No, I couldn't stay in ROTC. No, I hadn't been mistreated. No, I wasn't angry at him, or anybody. No, I was not against ROTC or the Air Force.
    All true, but all irrelevant, as I shrugged, and repeated the punch line: I just couldn't do it anymore.
    Hearing this, the colonel shifted gears and tried to look stern. "You know I can't just let you walk away," he barked. "I'll have to go through the process of throwing you out of the program. I'll have to write reports and say bad things about you."
    It was an unconvincing performance, but I didn't doubt

him. I nodded, and said it was too bad if that's what was required, but he would have to do what he had to do. He shook my hand when I left.

X

In relatively short order, the wheels of expulsion began to turn. I was called to a hearing before two sergeants, who asked me the same questions and made notes of my answers. Then a few weeks later I received another certified letter, containing a copy of their report.

It was very fair, duly noting that Cadet Fager had assured them he had no animosity toward the program or any individual, that his was a purely personal decision, etc. I would give a lot to have a copy of that report. With it was a letter signed by the Colonel, advising me that I had been "disenrolled" from ROTC, but this had been done "without prejudice." The prodigal could still return, if only I would.

XI

Almost thirty years later, in 1992, I was working for the Postal Service as a MailHandler in Virgina. One evening I was picking parcels, brochures and bulk mail out of a large hamper, when a thick paperback book came to hand. I glanced at the cover, thinking at first it must be a catalog of some sort.

Instead, it was the Alumni Directory for the US Air Force Academy. I stopped, moved quietly to a spot out of my supervisor's line of sight, and opened it up.

The book was organized chronologically, by class. I flipped quickly to the class of 1964. There, in alphabetical order, were thumbnail sketches of all that year's graduates.

A few were generals, but most had retired by now; several had died in plane crashes of various sorts, including combat in Vietnam. A significant number, it seemed, were now selling real estate as their second career.

This book presented a snapshot of what lay down the road not taken; it summarized the careers and lifepaths of the men I had almost joined, had almost become.

Reading the thumbnails made me thoughtful. These men, the survivors, received substantial pension checks each month;

they also probably received fundraising letters from their alma mater in Colorado Springs.

I recalled looking down at its shiny chapel from the T-38 with Major Bass.

Regret?

Not even a whisper.

Thirty years afterward, my reaction to Major Bass's declaration of devotion to flying – that I could think of several other things I'd rather do – still held.

And besides that, none of those guys had been to Selma, as far as I could see.

XII

The second messenger of Providence that autumn was my good buddy Dennis.

Dennis was big, ungainly and bespectacled, an earnest Lutheran kid from Denver. We met in Air Force ROTC my sophomore year, when I was commander of the drill team, and he tried out for it. On December 11, 1963, my 21st birthday, he was the one who took me to a bar in Fort Collins and insisted I order a drink – a hot buttered rum, as I recall – so I could flash my ID and be acknowledged as a man.

I followed his instructions, and got the proper rush from being street legal. But there was a catch – I didn't drink, then or now. At his urging, I sipped tentatively at the rum, grimaced at the taste, and quickly passed it to him. Dennis was a year younger, but he had considerably more familiarity with booze, and was happy to relieve me of this burden of age. The next day he presented me with a pipe, to complete my initiation into adult vice. I tried it a couple of times, but it burned my tongue and felt pretentious; I soon gave it up.

One habit Dennis and I did share was a passion for writing. His was of the more practical sort, however: where I edited the literary magazine and the yearbook, posts with no discernible future, he made a beeline for *The Collegian*, the campus daily. From there a diligent student might hope to graduate into a real job, writing for a real newspaper.

In that fateful autumn, he was its editor, and I was a weekly columnist. We often ended up hanging round *The Collegian*'s offices late at night, chewing the fat as the paper was put to bed.

It was on one of these nights, about the same time I quit ROTC, that Dennis lit a cigarette and picked up that morning's edition of the *Rocky Mountain News*, a Denver tabloid daily, to which at least one of his predecessors had graduated. Browsing desultorily through it, he suddenly sat up straight and said, "Hey, look at this."

I looked where he pointed. It was a small item, announcing that James Meredith would be in Denver soon, to speak to the local chapter of the NAACP.

By this time I had finally begun to notice the civil rights movement. It was the great 1963 March on Washington that did it; I listened, fascinated and apprehensive, as people around me confidently predicted that the gathering could not be held without violence and bloodshed. That didn't happen, of course; but then these dark prophecies were perversely confirmed a few days later, by the bombing of a Birmingham, Alabama church which killed four young girls.

I hadn't been paying attention two years earlier when James Meredith had integrated the University of Mississippi, amid gunfire and riots that cost two lives, brought out federal troops, and riveted world attention on the Magnolia State's peculiar cultural traditions. But I'd heard about it since, and was beginning to sense what I had missed.

"Jesus," I said, "I wish we could hear him." Then, "I wish we could get him up here."

I didn't add our oft-repeated complaint about CSU being a cultural desert and a hotbed of apathy, where even renowned public speakers drew small, indifferent audiences; I didn't have to.

But Dennis, the practical one, considered my statement thoughtfully for a moment, blowing smoke and flicking ashes on the floor. Then he said, "Why not give it a try?"

"How?" I asked. "Where do we find him?"

Dennis didn't know where, but he approached the problem like a good reporter. He called someone he knew at the News, who gave him a number for a Denver NAACP official. Soon Dennis had an address for Meredith in Mississippi. There was no phone number, so we split the cost of a telegram.

A few days later Dennis came rushing up to me, waving a pale yellow envelope. "We got a wire back!" he shouted. I snatched at it.

Meredith replied that he'd be glad to speak at CSU – for

$500 plus expenses.

My elation vanished. Five hundred dollars was a lot of money, and we didn't have it.

But Dennis wouldn't give up. After stewing over our plight for awhile, he proposed that we take the telegram to the student legislature, and ask them to underwrite the fee.

I was ready to go along, but felt some trepidation. I had served in the legislature, but the previous spring had left it to run for student body president, and lost in a landslide. We'd be taking our request to the same people who had defeated me.

On the other hand, what did we have to lose? We went, and made our best case to the skeptical solons: Meredith was a big name; his cause was just; and students would turn out. (We weren't really sure about this last.) We promised to charge fifty cents admission and return all proceeds to the student body treasury, recovering at least some portion of the $500.

Many of the leading lights were dubious, figuring that only the usual liberal handful would show, and it would be a waste of good student fee money. It looked like our idea was a non-starter.

But then the legislature's faculty adviser weighed in, and gave them a pep talk about not missing a chance to put CSU on the map. This was worth at least $500, he argued. As we listened, he basically shamed them into agreeing to it. Dennis and I were jubilant, and raced to send off another telegram to Mississippi.

We still worried about money, though. Meredith wanted $500 *plus expenses*. If the expenses included a motel room and meals, they could add up fast; and if the turnout was sparse, we could end up covering that portion ourselves. We needed some ways to save money.

Then I had a brainstorm: Meredith could stay at my fraternity house. Hosting an occasional overnight guest there was a perk of membership, and one I had never invoked before. He could eat there too, all on the house.

Dennis agreed: I was a genius.

XIII

It turned out there were to be a few hitches in my plan.

FarmHouse Fraternity, as the name indicates, was home mainly to students in agricultural fields, or from farm backgrounds.

I didn't fit either category, having grown up on military bases, and being a Humanities major. What drew me to FarmHouse was its reputation as a studious place: year after year it won the trophy for the highest overall grade average among the Greek houses. My grades, while not stellar, generally came in at or a bit above the house average, so I had held up my end. Also, before joining I had checked to see if our constitution included the racially exclusive clauses that were common in many other houses' charters; and it was clean. Not that this made a lot of difference on our nearly all-white campus; but I did want to know.

For two years I had lived in our house on South College Avenue peaceably enough, more or less accepted as something of an oddball, a familiar role for me. Some of my more rustic brethren never could see the point of my philosophy and honors English classes; but for that matter, I could not fathom how they could spend years immersed in Agronomy or Soils Science.

Just why I thought they would all be as thrilled as I to have James Meredith as a houseguest I can't now imagine. In any event, I was soon disabused of my ignorance.

First of all, this came up early in the year, during Rush, when the most promising freshman were being assiduously courted by the "better" fraternities. We were special rivals with the other agriculturally oriented house, Alpha Gamma Rho, at the other end of the campus. It was a close contest: we had the better grades, but they had a spiffy new building. Our officers had a list of the top rush prospects whom we hoped to attract. In this context, more than just a bed and a meal was involved in my unexpected invitation; our image was also in play.

Then there was the fact that some members came from places like South Dakota, where Negroes might be few and far between, but there were still persons of color to despise, especially Indians. And despise them they did, along with anyone who even faintly resembled them. I hadn't noticed this much; the subject hadn't come up often on our overwhelmingly white northern Colorado campus.

I began to suspect all was not well when I informed Ken, our chapter president, what was on my mind. Instead of simply nodding and passing this news along to the cook and our housemother, which was the usual procedure, this normally congenial fellow looked surprised and went off to consult with other officers. He came back to tell me that this idea needed to be brought to the chapter as a whole.

This was highly irregular; nobody else's guest had ever been thus examined. But the next day he announced that there would be an impromptu membership meeting as soon as we finished lunch.

Thus put on the spot, facing my brethren crowded into our living room, I told them what I had done: invited James Meredith to stay with us while he was here to speak on campus. Then I sat back and listened in growing astonishment and dismay as one brother after another rose to denounce the idea as, to quote the Birmingham ministers' letter to Dr. King, "unwise and untimely," to say the least. Most said it would be bad for our rush campaign; but a few even owned up to being personally unwilling to have us give shelter to a man of color.

Before I could make any response to this cascade of denunciation, someone offered a motion to withdraw my invitation of hospitality to Meredith, and it passed on a loud voice vote. The meeting then adjourned.

I was stunned. Wandering off to classes, I began composing a letter of resignation in my head, and wondering what Dennis and I were going to do. Book a motel room, probably, and dig ourselves into an even deeper financial hole. And of course we had to make sure Meredith didn't find out.

XIV

But as it happened, I was not alone in my chagrin. During the day, word about our action reached the office of the faculty advisor for fraternities. Unknown to me, he was soon on the phone to the house officers.

I can only imagine his message, but it must have been stern, and something like this:

You want to talk about reputation, fellas? Wait til the newspapers get hold of this story: James Meredith, after successfully desegregating the University of Mississippi, is refused hospitality at Colorado State University because of his race. Can you even imagine what this will mean for the university? For FarmHouse? Can you?

I suspect the message was reinforced by other university officials. But as I say, I knew nothing of this, and was surprised the next day when Ken rose at lunch, looking grave, and announced another, emergency chapter meeting.

Back in the crowded living room, I again listened, slack-jawed, as some of the same brothers who had most loudly criticized my proposal the day before, rose to announce that they had changed their minds – or rather, had been coerced into changing them.

One after another they angrily denounced unnamed persons, purveyors of slander and calumny, who had been working overtime, they said, to ruin the house's reputation on the campus. This conspiracy had succeeded in getting FarmHouse in very deep institutional trouble. Like a prairie fire, they insisted, it had to be stopped before it did any further damage.

If I didn't know yet what they were talking about, their withering looks made clear *who* was their prime suspect as the provocateur. Then one of the South Dakota brethren, who had been especially venomous, sullenly read a motion to reverse yesterday's action and re-extend the invitation to Meredith. The voice vote to pass it was just as loud as before, but much more surly in tone.

Naturally I was relieved, and as I learned of the support by university officials, gratified. But there wasn't much pleasure in this abrupt reversal. It was obvious that to a large number of my brethren, I was now *persona non grata* in my own house. And in fact, within a few months, I was to resign from the chapter, fed up with their harassment, and by then headed in a very different cultural direction. But that is another story.

XV

James Meredith came to CSU, he stayed at FarmHouse, and I don't think he ever suspected a thing. Our housemother was gracious and the brothers were polite, though there were several, I realized, who chose to find other quarters for the night he was there.

But the matter of hospitality was only one item on the agenda of preparations Dennis and I were dealing with. The most important task was to see if we could scare up enough of a turnout for the speech to avoid being publicly humiliated, not to mention left with the legislature thinking about dunning us for the deficit.

We soon resolved to make full use of the one resource we did have: access to the media. For a week before Meredith's arrival, Dennis saw to it that the Mississippian's coming was front-page news in the *Collegian*. I wrote a column about it. I also made a stack of large posters and stuck them up on every available bulletin board.

Such a publicity effort may sound rudimentary or obvious now; but on that campus, in that year, it was a nearly unprecedented blitz. Dennis and I pulled out all the stops; this, we knew, was our only chance.

And it worked. We had booked the ballroom of the Student Center, a room with movable partitions to divide it into three parts; we were set up for one third. But when Meredith, Dennis and I arrived, we found the entire ballroom opened and nearly filled. Something like 1500 people showed up.

This was the biggest turnout for a public speaker at CSU in anyone's memory. Dennis and I took seats on the platform, instant campus celebrities. The student legislature, to its utter incredulity, actually made money on the event.

Furthermore, Meredith proved very impressive at the podium. He was soft-spoken, and free of flights of oratory. He told us about growing up in Mississippi, serving a tour in the Air Force, and then returning home as a veteran who wanted a college degree, and looking to the Magnolia State's public university to get it. That this became a life-and-death struggle for him and the focus of world attention was not exactly what he had in mind; he did not come across as a crusader. But once his course was set, he saw it through, pitched battles, federal troops, and all.

The big ballroom grew very quiet as his story unfolded. It was very easy to identify with him: we were at a public university also, and many of us – myself included – were among the first generation in our families to go much beyond high school. Meredith could have been almost any of us; he could have been me.

Afterward, when we were driving him back to Denver, I asked him about black graduate schools; which one was the best?

Meredith's answer was immediate: "Atlanta University."

Let's make a long story short: the following September, I enrolled there.

Were these events just random? Was my life no more than a billiard ball, simply clacking and caroming around the green felt surface of history in 1963, and sent rolling toward the pocket marked "the movement" by accident? If all I had to report were these two nudges, it would be easy to think so; but there is more.

Chapter Four: Welcome to Atlanta

I

I lasted about three days as a graduate student. Atlanta University's catalog described its program of studies as being aimed at keeping up with "universities of highest standing," which in those waning pre-Black Power days meant elite white schools. As soon as I got to class, it became obvious that they meant it.

As an English major, one of my courses dealt with the 18th century British novel. The professor, a cultivated looking middle-aged black man, rolled into the classroom in a wheelchair, and immediately began lecturing urbanely about the development of fiction in England after the Restoration of Charles II. Our first assignment was to read Daniel Defoe's *A Journal of the Plague Year*. I obediently took the book home, to the small second floor apartment off Ponce de Leon Avenue I shared with Tish, my new wife.

But I couldn't concentrate on the reading. One set of problems was atmospheric: the radio regularly blared Martha and the Vandellas' hit, "Dancin' in the Streets," and described in painstaking detail the royal progress of the Beatles' national tour. The St. Louis Cardinals were closing in on an epic World Series clash with the Yankees. Also it was hot, and our windows were open all night. Through them, above the hum of our fan, we couldn't help listening as a gay couple next door alternately raged and talked sadomasochistic trash of a sort we had never heard or imagined before.

But all these distractions could have been managed. The real problem lay elsewhere: every newscast blared another unsettling report about the seemingly endless civil rights turmoil – three civil rights workers, two of them white college students, were dead in Mississippi, and all the evidence pointed to the local sheriff, who was thumbing his nose at the FBI. The Democrats' national political convention in Atlantic City had been shaken by the angry, eloquent dignity of Fanny Lou Hamer and her insurgent Mississippi Freedom Democrats. And in downtown Atlanta, a handful of merchants were making a doomed but determined stand against the new Civil Rights Act, and its ban on segregation in restaurants and other public facilities.

One such, The Pickrick Cafeteria run by Lester Maddox, was going for broke: when a federal court ordered it to admit blacks to its food line, Maddox declared defiantly that he would refuse to serve "integrationists" of whatever color. When this didn't fly, he pulled the pans of fried chicken and stewed vegetables off the steam tables, and replaced them with equally fiery stacks of engraved axhandles and segregationist tracts. Tish and I went to visit the Pickrick one weekend afternoon, and walked shocked and silent through the display, not knowing what to say or think about it all.

Maddox also trumpeted his defiance every week from large ads in the Atlanta Journal and Constitution. He was on his way to losing the legal battle, but paving the way thereby for an upstart political career that (one hopes) would be unimaginable today: Maddox later served as Governor of Georgia, and then hung on as Jimmy Carter's Lieutenant Governor and nemesis.

For most of its citizens, of course, life in Atlanta was going on pretty much as usual. But for me, a gawking newcomer, there was no escaping the signs of struggle and change. Every day I walked or rode past another restaurant, Leb's, which had closed its downtown location rather than serve blacks. Big brightly-lettered posters hung in the windows, denouncing integration, Lyndon Johnson, and civil rights generally.

But more startling was the entirely routine tableau, unnoticed by natives, that I came upon riding the bus into town early one morning. At the central bus transfer station, in a narrow street between two blocks of high-rise buildings, huge crowds of somber black women, wearing cloth coats and clutching large handbags, jammed the long transfer islands, waiting for buses to the suburbs.

I caught my breath as I realized what they were: maids, almost every one of them, headed out to their middle-class Missus' houses for a long day's work, cooking white meals, cleaning white floors and bathrooms, and minding white children. I saw them again late in the day, gathered on the same islands but facing the opposite direction, making their weary return trips. Their tired, stoic faces haunted me.

As far as I could tell, Atlanta University was staying out of all this civil rights hullabaloo, sticking to its work of keeping up with (white) schools "of highest standing." I had no reason to complain, though; it had also welcomed me, with a fellowship that covered most of my tuition. But Daniel Defoe never stood a chance of holding my attention in the face of this steady onslaught of change.

Within a few days, I had admitted to myself, as I had with ROTC, "I can't do this." Not knowing what my alternatives were, about a week after that first class, I paid a call on the university's courtly, gray-haired president in his office to yield back my fellowship, and then dropped out.

II

For the next several weeks, I wrestled with destiny, in the form of a rather self-important question:

Obviously, I felt, I had been drawn to the South to play some role in the civil rights movement. But what?

More specifically, I saw two possible options: On the one hand, to be a reporter chronicling the action; and on the other, to plunge into it as an activist civil rights worker.

How to decide which path to take?

Let me acknowledge that I agonized over this grand life-decision without benefit of a job offer, or even a contact, in either field. For that matter, I also lacked a degree. I had come up one credit short in art the previous spring at CSU, had taken a ceramics course in summer school, and flunked it flat.

Now, for several weeks I had no paying work at all; I left the task of earning our meager keep to Tish, who wound up running the switchboard for a textile company. This period was hardly my finest hour as a respecter of gender equality. Tish was very magnanimous to put up with me, and she did not always do it gladly.

Which is not to say that I was completely idle. In fact, I soon began writing what became a series of feature articles about the wonders and horrors of my new home–describing Lester Maddox and the Pickrick axhandles was a particular pleasure. I sent these off to *The Collegian* back in Colorado. They were duly published, and spoken of highly by my contacts there. But of course they didn't pay anything.

By the same token, it wasn't strictly accurate to say I was

not looking for a job. I was quite willing to work for, say, *Time* or *Newsweek*, and even enlisted an energetic counselor at a downtown employment agency to pass on this wonderful news to my selected outlets. Unfortunately, their Atlanta bureaus failed to leap at my generous offer. Then I turned to the broadcast media, and actually landed an interview with the News Director at WSB, the premier local station. That didn't pan out either.

The employment agency's last, noblest effort was to uncover an opening for a reporter at the *Anniston Star*, across the border in eastern Alabama. I rode a Greyhound over there, trembling with excitement. It was near Anniston, I had just recently learned, that a bus carrying an integrated group of Freedom Riders had been burned and its passengers beaten in 1961. The *Star* had shown courage in reporting on these events and denouncing racism. But perhaps because of this experience, the editor who talked with me couldn't see the value of taking on a wet-behind-the-ears rookie from the North, and no job materialized.

After Anniston, the employment agency's interest in me cooled; I was too picky for the jobs they actually had, and for the ones I wanted I was, to put it charitably, not ready. There were a few desperate days: at one point we pawned the high fidelity record player that was Tish's pride and joy; then I even ventured down to Atlanta's skid row and sold a pint of blood for five dollars. Tish's patience with my existential angst was wearing thin; we needed money, and I needed some direction.

At one point I responded to an ad for encyclopedia salesmen. The Sales Director was a hearty sort, who assembled me and several other newcomers in his office for a peptalk about all the money we could make, and how easy it was to make it: just talk to people on the phones, and then show the prospects the wonderful informative books. He presented us with shiny new briefcases full of samples and sales materials. Then he passed out sheets of names and phone numbers, and walked us down the hall to another room where a bank of dingy booths with phones were waiting. We could start, he said, right now.

I sat down in a booth, contemplating the phone and the list of names, and waves of panic began washing over me. I may have actually made one or two calls, but scarcely more, before suddenly recalling an urgent appointment and scurrying out of the building, leaving my shiny new briefcase behind. No one tried to stop me; I imagine the Sales Director had witnessed many such hurried, tail-between-the-legs departures.

It was after this fiasco that I decided I might be willing to start my work on behalf of humanity more humbly, laboring in the vineyards of the local press, especially the city's big daily, the Atlanta *Constitution*.

The *Constitution* was famous as a progressive-minded southern paper, whose publisher, Ralph McGill, had won a Pulitzer Prize for his editorial stands against segregation and the Klan. He still wrote, and I carefully read, a daily column which ran down the left side of the paper's front page.

Yes, such an institution might meet my minimum professional requirements. I'd even be willing to start at the bottom. I had seen classified ads for copy boys in the paper, and as the weeks passed, began to adjust to the idea, as a way of gaining a foothold.

We soon escaped the apartment off Ponce de Leon, and found a tiny bungalow behind a house in the far northeast, a long busride from downtown.

One place we looked for solace and enlightenment during these difficult weeks was church. Specifically, Atlanta's Unitarian congregation, which was meeting in a school until their own building was finished.

Why the Unitarians? Much later I read a remark by the wife of the Supreme Court justice Oliver Wendell Holmes, when asked the same question: "In Boston," she said, "you had to be something, and Unitarian was the *least* you could be."

Something like that applied for me at this point; like my guru Jung, I was not interested in joining up with one of the creedal churches. But religion was still a major interest, and we also needed a social network to connect with. I didn't know much about Unitarians beyond the fact that they had no formal creed, and that was enough for a start.

On one fateful Sunday, the minister had us sing the hymn, "Once to Every Man and Nation," with lyrics by James Russell Lowell.

These verses are familiar enough to American Protestants; but coming out of my pre-Vatican II youth, when most Catholic hymns were sung in Latin, they were brand new to me, and struck like a bolt of lightning:

> "Once to every man and nation
> Comes the moment to decide

In the strife of truth with falsehood
For the good or evil side.
Some great cause, some great decision
Offering each the bloom or blight
And the choice goes by forever
'Twixt that darkness and that light.

By the light of burning martyrs
Christ Thy bleeding feet we track.
Toiling up new Calvaries ever
With the cross that turns not back.
New occasions teach new duties
Time makes ancient good uncouth.
They must upward still and onward
Who would keep abreast of truth."

(Actually, I suspect that the Unitarian hymnbook edited out the part about Christ and new Calvaries; but I don't have that volume to refer to, so these are the original.)

Giddy with a mix of callowness and idealism, I stumbled out of that service convinced I had heard the word of a God I didn't even believe in. It was time to decide, to get off the dime.

Perhaps reporting on the civil rights struggle wasn't to be my path. Maybe the moment called for a plunge directly into the movement.

I went home, unlimbered my small portable typewriter, and banged out a series of letters announcing my availability to the main civil rights groups: The NAACP, the Student Nonviolent Coordinating Committee (SNCC), the Urban League, and Dr. King's group, the Southern Christian Leadership Conference (SCLC). I proposed to be a writer for them, reporting to the world their efforts on behalf of justice and equality.

Amazingly, over the next few weeks the groups actually took the time to respond, in what I soon came to understand were their characteristic organizational styles: the Urban league and NAACP sent employment application forms, and referred me impersonally to their national offices. Someone at SNCC, which was already seething with the nationalist ferment that later emerged under the slogan "Black Power," sent a curt brushoff, which made it plain they didn't need any more self-important white kids cluttering up their offices. These replies were discouraging, yet both predictable and entirely justified.

But then a letter appeared in our box from Mr. Randolph Blackwell, the Program Director of SCLC. Opening the envelope, I could see that the message was brief, and restrained my hopes; probably just another polite turndown.

"Dear Mr. Fager," it began, "Your letter was received here with delight."

The autumn afternoon suddenly turned incandescent. Blackwell went on to say that SCLC was looking for an in-house staff writer, and invited me to call him at my early convenience to discuss the possibility of working in such a capacity.

Be still my heart! And recalling that white sheet of stationery, the query rises again, as it did then: is there such a thing as Providence? If so, its breath stirred through that letter like the wind that bloweth where it listeth in the third chapter of the Gospel of John. I knew it as sure as I was standing there.

There was only one problem:

When Blackwell's letter came, I already had a job.

III

An ad for a copy boy had appeared in the morning paper not long before. I had raced downtown the same day to apply in person. The slot was not, alas, for the *Constitution*, but for its less-renowned afternoon sister, the Atlanta *Journal*. Both were housed in the same building downtown, the result of an early example of media mergers. Before long a dignified News Editor was looking over his half-eyeglasses at me, a brash young Yankee, and pursing his lips thoughtfully. After reviewing my college record, he decided I was worth a try, at $1.25 per hour.

A copy boy's duties centered around a bank of black wire service ticker machines in the newsroom. The tickers hummed steadily, and emitted a spasmodic but endless stream of yellow fanfold copy paper. Each machine had a little bell, which let out tinny dings whenever an article was coming; the more dings, the more urgent the story

It was my task to listen for the dings, tear off the lengths of paper, sort the articles roughly by topic, and drop them into wire baskets on various editors' and reporters' desks. Beyond that, I was a gofer, running errands, getting coffee, and whatnot.

This hardly measured up to my exalted view of my capabilities and prospects. But it was a start, and there was the clear sense that I could work my way up to be a reporter and maybe someday an editor; others had risen from similarly humble origins. My paycheck, trifling as it was, pulled us back from the brink: Tish's record player came back from the pawnshop, and I forgot about selling more blood.

More to my liking, my hero-of-the-moment Ralph McGill was not far away; in fact, his name was painted on the door of an upper floor office. I walked past there as often as possible, though I never actually laid eyes on the eminent occupant.

The job had other compensations as well, above all the chance to learn about news stories that others didn't see. One day I ripped a long piece from the ticker which was datelined Berkeley, California. It described in detail the student uprising that soon became known as the Free Speech Movement, and mentioned a name I still revere, that of its spontaneous, emblematic spokesman, Mario Savio.

"Wow," I said to the News Editor, "get a load of this. These guys are really on to something."

But the News Editor frowned and harumphed as he scanned the yellow sheets. Evidently he did not share my enthusiasm for Yankee student protest, and the story did not appear in the paper. Thus it began to dawn on me that the *Journal-Constitution*'s reputation as a progressive southern institution was a relative thing. The paper, it seemed, was not in the business of reporting militant social activism, except when, as in the local civil rights demonstrations, it had no real choice. For that matter, I soon noticed that the building's restrooms were still segregated, which bothered me, and that all the newsroom staff I saw, including me, were white.

Nonetheless, I hearkened to the News Editor's cue, and kept my mouth shut as more stories from Berkeley came cascading from the tickers in the next weeks. But I read as many as I could, and probably knew more about the Free Speech Movement than most people in Georgia.

Like many others my age who also read them, these stories were not only a matter of information; the shouts of students crowded around a police car in California stirred something deep in me, increased my dissatisfaction with what I knew of the world's status quo. Among other effects, their shouts, which it somehow seemed I could hear even though I only read about them, also kept me from forgetting about Randolph Blackwell's letter.

IV

One day I slipped out at lunch, called the SCLC office, and made an appointment. Before long, another lunch hour found me sitting across from Mr. Blackwell in his crowded office on Auburn Avenue.

Blackwell was a tall rumpled, chain smoker, who welcomed me cordially. Yes, he said, they had need of an in-house writer to produce articles, brochures and news releases, and I looked like just the one who could do this. I assured him I was.

So did we have a deal? I was eager. The SCLC offices, crowded and small as they were, felt infinitely more exciting, more real somehow, than the staid *Journal* newsroom. Blackwell smiled enigmatically, pulled on his cigarette, and said he supposed so.

But of course there was a catch. All he could offer me by way of pay was the rate for what SCLC called a "subsistence worker," $25 per week. That was about half of what I was getting at the *Journal*; and even though Tish and I were living fairly simply, it still wasn't much. I held out for $60 a week.

Blackwell smiled again, lit another cigarette, and said he thought that was unlikely, but he'd see what he could do. We agreed to keep in touch.

We did, even though Blackwell soon reported that the subsistence worker's rate was indeed the most I could hope for on SCLC's payroll. At the beginning of December, I paid another visit to the SCLC offices, just to keep my name before them. As I came in, there was a sense of bustle and excitement. Turning into the narrow hallway to Blackwell's office, I ran into a line of several men in dark suits and overcoats.

Then my breathing stopped: in the lead was Dr. King himself.

Heart in my throat, I stepped forward and introduced myself. He shook my hand, smiled, and said hello in that unmistakable voice. He and his entourage were just leaving, headed for New York and Oslo, where he was to be awarded the Nobel Peace Prize. Then he and they waved and headed out the door. It was over in a moment.

Watching them go, my initial reaction was shock, at the staggering realization that Dr. Martin Luther King, Jr. – the new Moses, one of the towering public figures of our time, the Nobel Laureate – yes, *that* Dr. King, was shorter than me.

Not by much. But there I was, gazing down slightly at his retreating figure.

V

Dr. King would be gone for two weeks. But was more going on in the SCLC office than the hubbub over the Oslo trip, exciting as that was. I learned that two other major plans were in the works: one was something called the "Alabama Project," which I gathered was to center on a nationwide boycott, aimed at forcing the state to end discrimination in voting and other areas. More immediately, Dr. King had agreed to support a local labor strike.

My ears perked up when I heard about these schemes. Surely there would be stories to be written about them, and of course I'd seen and heard nothing about either at the *Journal*. Maybe I could even get the paper to let me write about one of them, make them the vehicle for my debut as a cub reporter. I liked that idea.

The strike was more accessible; it was local, and was already on. Someone soon filled me in: There was a Scripto Pen Company plant not far from the SCLC offices, in the heart of a black neighborhood. Its several hundred production workers were divided into two categories, skilled and unskilled.

The union contended that the actual division was not a matter of skill, but race. All the workers did pretty much the same tasks; but all of the few hundred "skilled" workers except a handful were white, while the much larger group of "unskilled" workers was black, and mainly women to boot. These women, some of whom had been there for ten or more years, earned only $1.25 per hour – the same as me. Word was that most of the "skilled" whites had learned their jobs from "unskilled" black co-workers.

With the coming of the civil rights movement, the black women at Scripto became increasingly restive, and finally contacted the International Chemical Workers Union. They won a union election, and in late November, when the company refused to recognize the union, they walked out. A number of them were also members of Ebenezer Baptist Church, where Dr. King Sr., "Daddy King," was pastor and Dr. King, Jr. his assistant and heir. The church women went to Daddy King, and soon both Kings were on board.

Reading in the *Journal* about Dr. King's triumph in Oslo kept me alert to the movement, and made the newsroom's enforced calm feel increasingly restrictive. As December went on, the Scripto strike also showed no signs of resolution. Management at first offered raises of two per cent for unskilled and four per cent for skilled workers, and professed shock and amazement when the strikers reacted with outrage at the disparity. Then they offered an across the board raise of four cents an hour, which was likewise met with derision. All the while the company ran ads in the city's papers for replacement workers. At the bottom of each ad was the self-mocking line, "An equal Opportunity Employer."

Dr. King returned to Atlanta on December 18. Blackwell passed on the news that Dr. King planned to walk the picket line with the strikers, and was talking about organizing an international boycott of Scripto to pressure the company into resolving the strike. I also learned that there was to be a mass meeting in a black church not far from the plant, to show solidarity and plan the next steps, and Dr. King was scheduled to address it.

This information was the signal to make a move to reporting at the *Journal*. I went to the News editor, told him what I had learned, and begged for the chance to report on the meeting. I was even willing to do it on my own time.

The News Editor took off his horn-rimmed glasses and scratched his head. The body language suggested some of the same irritation that the Free Speech Movement evoked; but on the other hand, this was local; it was news, sure enough.

He looked up at me and frowned. "How did you hear about this anyway?" he drawled.

Ummm. On guard, I mumbled some evasion, not about to admit that I was practically moonlighting for Randolph Blackwell. Not in that newsroom anyhow. But the editor was not overly irritated; he was also impressed with my initiative. Maybe he'd been a copy boy himself once. He understood the cub's desire to get out there and get the news.

Sensing his ambivalence, I pressed. "Come on," I pleaded. "I can do this." It was no big deal: sit there, listen to the speeches, take some notes, write them up. Piece of cake.

Finally the News Editor frowned, and made a decision. He called to one of the other reporters, who came obediently to his desk. "King is gonna preach about this Scripto strike," he said. "Fager here wants to cover it, and I'll let him. But I want you to be there too, and be ready to write it up just in case."

Having a backup did not offend me. I was, after all, untested. And I was confident I could write up the speech as well as any reporter there; better even. This was going to be my big break; I just knew it.

VI

December darkness came early on the evening of the rally, and my familiarity with Atlanta geography was only enough to get me within sight of the Scripto plant. Once that landmark was in view, I realized I had no clue where the church was in relation to it.

I walked uncertainly along the sidewalk on one side of the plant, then turned a corner and headed toward its main gate. By the gate there were several black women, bundled up against the chill, bearing large picket signs and walking slowly toward me in single file.

They would know! As the one in the lead approached, I walked over to her, smiled and asked courteously, "Uh, excuse me ma'am, but could you tell me where–"

She looked at me, through me, and walked right past, solid,

implacable, and utterly silent.

At first I was confused. I had been as polite as I knew how to be. But the others trudged by just as impassively.

At the gate, though, a strike captain was willing to answer my question. Both of them: where the church was, and why the silent treatment. The latter was simplicity itself: picket line discipline. Picketers did not speak to any stranger. Why should they, especially a white stranger? The strikebreaking provocateur, sent to provoke disruption and violence to be blamed on the strikers, was a staple of union lore. Then I felt foolish and green, but learning fast.

The church was only a few blocks away. When I came in, it was about half-filled, and I recognized some of the SCLC office staff among them. In fact, they were leading the group in singing, clapping rhythmically for accompaniment. They were singing Freedom songs: "Ain't Gonna Let Nobody Turn Me Round," "Woke Up This Morning With My Mind Stayed On Freedom," and others.

I had heard about these Freedom songs, but had not actually heard them before. And it is impossible to overstate the effect of the music, and the spirit which produced it. Looking back, even a few months later, I would know that the singing was in part a way of filling the time, keeping things going while, up around the pulpit, the pastor and a couple of Dr. King's close aides huddled, figuring out what to do next.

But on their own, in that time, sung by those people, they had an impact that was both visceral and transcendent. I sat down on a bench, nodded to my backup reporter in another part of the church, and let the music carry me away.

Finally, after a few more songs, Hosea Williams stood and put up his hands to quiet us, then stepped to the pulpit. Hosea was from across the state in Savannah, where he had led an aggressive voter registration campaign and served time in jail for it. He was the newest addition to Dr. King's inner circle. Besides a natural eloquence, Hosea had a wonderful gift of perspiration. No matter that it was December, as soon as he began to preach, he also began to sweat, profusely, the drops sliding down his square cheeks, his large white handkerchief in hot pursuit.

I don't remember what he preached about; it must have had

to do with Scripto, and freedom, and justice, and the need to keep on keeping on. And after him another staffer preached also, on similar topics. They were followed by more singing, more of that irresistible, transforming music.

And then, with a round of "We Shall Overcome," the meeting was over, people were leaving, and through the haze of exaltation, I gradually realized that Dr. King had not appeared.

I saw my backup reporter talking to Hosea, then he came toward me. He shrugged, told me that Dr. King was often a no-show, that was the breaks, and then he left also.

Without King of course, there was no story, so there went my debut in the columns of the *Journal*

I should have been disappointed, but I wasn't. In fact, after a bit of reflection I was relieved. The mass meeting had been something of a bust as mass meetings went: a middling crowd, middling preaching, no Dr. King, and no noteworthy pronouncements. I'm not sure I had even taken any notes.

But for me the evening delivered much more than news; it brought revelation.

I had come into the church still thinking of myself as properly cast in the role of the reporter, an Olympian observer, reporting on and analyzing these events, much as I had in my report to the *Collegian* on Lester Maddox and his Pickrick.

I left the building quite clear that this was not my path, at least not now: the music, the preaching, and what they expressed, were like the burning bush on Sinai, the manifestation of something I had to be a part of, to the extent that I could; there was no other way for me; not then.

The next day on my lunch hour, I found a pay phone outside the *Journal* building and called Blackwell. "All right," I told him, "if $25 a week is all you can pay, I'll take it. When can I start?"

We agreed on the following Monday. I sleepwalked through the rest of that week, ripping the yellow sheets from the ticker machines, getting the editors their coffee, and watching the clock, all in something of a daze. On Friday, after the late editions came out and my shift was up, I walked out of the *Journal* office without giving notice, and never returned.

Chapter Five
Struck Dumb

I

I arrived at the SCLC office reputed to be a writer, ready and able to churn out usable copy on behalf of Dr. King and the movement, as I had done for the *Collegian*.

Now I had the chance to show my stuff; and almost from the first day, I blew it.

For one thing, I proved to be a technical incompetent: asked to make some calls to other cities to gather some information, I seemed unable to make the office WATS line work. A WATS line was a flat-rate long distance line: one used it by dialing in a special number, the equivalent of a PIN today, and could then call anywhere at no additional toll charges. I'd never seen such a marvel before, couldn't get the hang of dialing into it, and was embarrassed to keep asking the secretaries to help me.

Next I was asked to design and lay out a new brochure about SCLC. I fretted over what kind of type face to use; I knew nothing of graphics, and in this pre-word processing era, comparing type fonts was not such a simple matter. At my boss's suggestion, I visited a local print shop to get some samples. The printer was happy to oblige, running off my test copy in a dozen or two different styles, as I studiously compared and worried over which one to select. Then he billed SCLC for about $200, a huge sum for such a purpose. Blackwell's reproof, when he saw the invoice, was gentle and patient.

My immediate boss was Ed Clayton, Dr. King's Information Director. Mr. Clayton was a large, balding man with a deep voice, who had been some kind of distinguished writer-editor before coming to SCLC. He was always well-turned out, in a bow tie, starched dress shirt and black suspenders, and presided over my fumbling efforts from behind a huge desk which dwarfed his small office He was patient with my inexperience, or at least he seemed to be.

It wasn't long, though, before I realized that patience was less a factor in his supervision than distraction. By early afternoon, I discovered, Clayton was usually drunk: unobtrusively but thoroughly inebriated, slurring his words, swaying when he gestured, fit for not much more than dozing at his desk.

Everybody else, of course, knew this, and quietly detoured around his office most of the day. Dr. King tolerated the situation, whether out of denial, pity or some sense of loyalty I never figured out. But Clayton's condition, while it relieved me of wrath over my bumbling, also left me without any useful guidance. No wonder SCLC had needed the help with writing Blackwell had spoken of when he hired me! But between Clayton's alcoholic disability and my green inability, the department was not very productive.

In search of something I could handle, I went back to Blackwell for help. He puffed on his cigarettes and smiled enigmatically, apparently understanding the whole situation at a glance. There was, he said, another project I could work on, and quietly report to him about, as well as keeping up appearances with Mr. Clayton: an article commissioned by *Ebony* Magazine, on "The Men Around Dr. King." Although it would be put into final form by *Ebony's* staff writers, they wanted us to furnish reports of interviews with all Dr. King's Executive Staff; and I could do that, Blackwell said.

This sounded promising, even exciting. I told Clayton about it that afternoon, and he just nodded extravagantly, probably barely hearing what I was saying. The next morning, I set out to do my first interview, which also turned out to be my last.

II

Perhaps appropriately, first on the list of "the men around Dr. King," was a woman: Mrs. Septima Poinsette Clark. This was more logical than I realized, because Mrs. Clark, being female, was at the bottom of the status ladder of what was called the Executive

Staff, and thus the most accessible.

Yet, being female, Mrs. Clark's place in Dr. King's orbit was not as straightforward as it appeared. She had come to SCLC from a project in Tennessee that had developed a program of Citizenship Education, which taught illiterate adult sharecroppers how to read. The course dealt less with ABCs than showing them how to understand such documents of survival as bank accounts, which most of them had never had, and aspiration: the Bill of Rights, which few had even heard of. This program, which also trained many of its students to become teachers themselves, went on without fanfare or public notice. But it was nevertheless profoundly subversive of both the outward and the inward pillars of Southern racism.

Mrs. Clark was herself a calm pillar of the movement, whose roots were sunk deep in its past: she had, I learned, joined the NAACP before World War One, when the group was new and radical. And she did so in South Carolina, which was about as tough a place as there was in the Deep South.

Moreover, she had been a schoolteacher, of the sort who could control a room full of unruly youth without raising her voice. I often wondered if she played a similar role in executive staff meetings; she had the presence, and that gaggle of seething male egos surely needed her steadying influence as much as any group she had ever been in.

Just how quietly imposing Mrs. Clark could be became massively evident almost as soon as I sat down in her small office and introduced myself. I think I began taking notes of our conversation, but I soon stopped, and they are lost. At home that night, I sat down at the typewriter, rolled in a sheet of paper, and tried to write about what had happened.

But instead of a draft profile, all that would come out of my fingers was, of all things, a poem. That I still have, and it is worth reproducing here:

On Meeting Mrs. Septima Poinsette Clark
Atlanta, December 9, 1964

I sit down quietly in the *chair*,
The older woman smiles and light
Reflects off frame glasses and gold rose earrings, the voice
Is like, is like the whisper of tires on a faroff nighttime highway
Or maybe that of a Negro woman of sixty-six
Which it is.
She inhales to speak, I raise
My fine young journalistic pen, prepared to summarize
Her story into ink traces,
To finish my entry blank in the Biographical Sweepstakes:
"Tell us, in 150 words or less,
The substance of her life"; I am, of course, confident—
The smile fades back into equilibrium, and she says calmly:
"My Father was a slave."
I see, yes—the pen moves to the paper:
M-Y-F-A-T-H-E-R-W-A-S-A-S-L-A—
Ahh, ha ha ha,
No, something isn't quite right,
She didn't even blink.
Voice steady *My Father*— Hands quiescent in her lap
    My Father— Breathing is regular
    My Father— Oh no.
You see, my father was a normal, middle-class guy like
    everybody else,
You understand that don't you Mrs.
    — *My Father was*
Yes, Yes, I know, but surely you can understand the difference was
    only superficial, just an accident of history that yours
    happened to be

— *a slave* (why in hell won't she blink)
Well it was his own damn fault, wasn't it—after all he must have known the Truth, because
My Father was
The Good Book, you know, says that
Ye shall know the Truth, and the Truth shall make you—
—a slave.
Say that's kind of a clever twist there Mrs.— Ahh, ha ha ha. . . .
Lay down your pen and sniffle for shame, boy— You there, the intellectual snot-nose,
Mucus running from your pen and you
With the cheek to call it ink.
But then, you have been to a university and so of course you know all about slavery
You even wrote a thousand-word paper on it (for extra credit, that is)
". . . . .basically a part of the economic system, the indispensable supply
Of cheap labor for the harvesting of the cotton crop. . . ."
But you missed the chapter in the non-required readings about how to face a calm old woman who can look you in your smooth white face and say
—My Father
And not even blink you say could you talk just a little slower please *ma'am*
I didn't get that last part your father was a what
—a slave.
Just like my father except for one or two of those little accidents of History, heh heh
My aren't we an
educated magnanimous liberal christian, boy
— Go to the rear of the
class, get out the dictionary and look up the following six words

71

then write for the next three hundred years after school is out on the new whiteboard with the black chalk the following sentence which you may have run across some where in your supplementary extracurricular living:

"My father was not a slave,"

That's it, only at the end,

Put a question mark.

III

The stunning encounter with Mrs. Clark pretty much put an end to the plan of writing a series of profiles for *Ebony*. Not that it was a bad idea; what was mistaken was the notion that I was the one to do it. She showed me, serenely and without rebuke, how presumptuous it was for me to be in any such position of explaining what was going on in the SCLC office, or out in the tides of personal and social change which kept it afloat.

I didn't give up, however. Near Mrs. Clark's office was a new one for Hosea Williams. Hosea was hard at work on a lengthy grant proposal; some northern foundation was ready to give him, through SCLC, the huge sum of $250,000 to run a region-wide project the coming summer. Hosea had christened it SCOPE, for Summer Community Organizing and Political Education, and he had big ambitions for it.

There was more than a touch of intra-movement rivalry in the impetus for SCOPE. Just months before, the Mississippi Freedom Summer had produced seemingly nonstop bombshell headlines, along with a string of violent incidents capped by the murder of three civil rights workers, that had shaken the country. But SCLC had had little presence in Mississippi. The Project there had been run mainly by SNCC, leaving Dr. King and SCLC very much on the sidelines of that titanic struggle. SCOPE, Hosea hoped (Dr. King too?), would recapture the spotlight and momentum for SCLC, while spreading the contagion of freedom among blacks all across the region.

One morning I was called in to look over part of the draft of the grant proposal. I walked into Hosea's office feeling confident: this was different than my humbling session with Mrs. Clark. This was about text, and I did know something about editing text; I'd have the proposal whipped into shape in no time.

Again I misjudged the situation. But given the mix of race and testosterone, this meeting was utterly different: Hosea seemed to me more interested in editorial approval than editorial input, and we did not hit it off. Soon we were shouting disagreements over the weighty issue of whether such a term as "delimited" (which he, the scientist, preferred) was better than "limited" (my liberal arts type's favorite) in a paragraph outlining the range of SCOPE's plans. The discussion didn't get much further.

I soon retreated; after all, it was his project. But in the course of this session I learned about other schemes which were also coming down SCLC's pipeline. The most notable of these was a nascent plan for a nationwide boycott of Alabama, aimed at forcing state officials to permit more blacks to register. This Alabama Project was taking shape under the aegis of another member of the Executive Staff, James Bevel.

As soon as I heard about the "Alabama Project," I was intrigued; and when I met Bevel, I was spellbound. Bevel was short, serious-looking, and charismatic. He stood out among the suits of the other Executive Staff members, because he wore the movement field uniform of overalls all the time, though with carefully starched and pressed dress shirts beneath them. He also shaved his head, an unheard of practice in those days, and covered it with a colorful, elaborately beaded yarmulke, which I gathered came from Africa. His voice was high and almost squeaky, but he had a natural eloquence and energy that was very magnetic.

The more I learned about the Alabama Project, the more it appealed to me. Besides the boycott, it included plans for demonstrations, and mass arrests. The town of Selma, fifty miles west of the Capital in Montgomery, had been chosen for this "direct action" phase, which, I was informed, was to start in a few weeks.

I had never heard of Selma and knew little of the state, beyond my brief visit to Anniston in search of a reporting job. But Alabama was rich in the civil rights lore I was rapidly absorbing. After the Freedom Riders had been attacked near Anniston in 1961, they patched and bandaged their wounds, managed to get another bus and made it a few hours farther south to Montgomery, where they were brutally attacked again.

James Bevel, then a Tennessee college student, had rallied several classmates to take up their pilgrimage in Montgomery, and made it to Mississippi, where they were jailed for their trouble.

Then, in 1963, had come the frenzy of the Birmingham campaign. It brought the shameful spectacle of police turning fire hoses and dogs on peaceful demonstrators to the world's TV screens, produced Dr. King's Letter from a Birmingham Jail, and was followed by the Klan bombing of the Sixteenth street Baptist Church in which four young girls were killed. If I had been oblivious to all this at the time, I knew better now.

Whatever Dr. King's final plans turned out to be, Alabama clearly demanded the movement's attention. But the Project's most important feature, as far as I was concerned, was simply that it was, in office argot, "out in the field," that is, away from Atlanta.

Even after only a couple of weeks, I had realized that the SCLC office was, well, an office – a necessary part of the movement infrastructure no doubt, but taken up with office routines and paperwork. I had also met big James Orange, a tall, beefy but genial movement veteran. Orange lived "in the field," and regarded all of us in the Atlanta office with the polite skepticism of the grizzled line officer for the pampered, office-bound general staff. He was friendly, but told me that if I really wanted to be "in the movement," I needed to get "out in the field," and "pay some dues."

I knew Orange was right. "Out in the field" was where "the movement" was actually in motion; where demonstrations were organized, and people were facing police dogs, jail, bombs and Klan riders. Out there it was dangerous, exciting, unpredictable.

It was, forgive the inescapable cliche, where the action was. And as much as I was learning on Auburn Avenue, I was not satisfied with relating to what was happening at one remove; I was no more cut out to fit into the office routine of SCLC headquarters than I was that of the Atlanta *Journal*.

With each passing December day, I felt more strongly that "the field" was where I wanted, where I needed to be. I told Bevel this. I also told Blackwell.

Despite my numerous missteps, Blackwell was reluctant to let me go. But he had been young once, and understood. He listened to my plea, smiled enigmatically behind his cigarettes, and finally told me he'd let me visit Selma for the first round of marches, provided I filed daily dispatches by phone to Atlanta, summarizing events for the office to use in fielding press queries. I eagerly agreed.

When I told Tish about this, she was also reluctant, but she too could see I was determined. For that matter, she wanted to go along. That wasn't immediately possible, because she was still working as a telephone operator-receptionist at the textile company. I said we'd figure something out.

Soon enough, I was advised that the Alabama campaign was to be kicked off with a rally in Selma the day after New years, January 2, 1965.

By dawn that morning, I had wangled an office airline ticket, and worried my way through the brief flight to Montgomery, and then the ride west from there, on U.S. Highway 80, through the brushy barrenness of Lowndes County. After about an hour, the rusty arches of the Edmund Pettus Bridge loomed ahead, crossing above the Alabama River into Selma. The city's small three-story business district huddled against the bluff overlooking the river. Here was "the field" for certain.

We made our way to Brown Chapel, where a large crowd was milling around outside, and more were packed into the crescent-shaped benches inside. Soon I was being carried on the tide of exultant resistance in a full-fledged, full-throated mass meeting.

I don't recall what Dr. King or anyone else said from the pulpit, except for Dr. King's peroration, built around rhythmic repetitions of the phrase, "Give us the ballot!" each answered by a swelling chorus. The crowd seemed as amazed as I was that such an event could be happening right in their midst.

At a staff meeting afterward, everyone was exuberant. Each movement campaign was much like a theatrical production, and on that day, the opening of SCLC's Alabama production had been a smash. Again and again, someone in the circle called out, "I believe we're gonna have a *move*ment here in Selma," and each time Dr. King chuckled quiet agreement. I clapped along, wondering how I had managed to stumble into such exalted, historic company.

Soon enough, of course, I was also discovering their flaws and weaknesses: Dr. King and others in his circle were womanizers; all kinds of personality clashes and rivalries were afoot. Nor was I to be entirely free of these temptations and failings. These discoveries could be painful; they were certainly frustrating. And cumulatively, they were slowly eating away at SCLC's morale and effectiveness.

But on the other hand, the day of reckoning was still far off; the compound interest of time on these failings had yet to accumulate to a critical mass. Even then, however, I had a sense that our sins were mostly those of weakness and appetite, rather than the heart and soul. That is to say, the movement then had a core of integrity: Dr. King, who was then at its center, may have yielded to sensual pleasures frequently. But at the same time he was not in the movement for sex, or money, or political power. Moreover, whatever happened late some nights, every day he also put his life on the line, as did many others.

It is a hard thing to say, but I often think the assassin's bullet in Memphis was a very severe mercy for Dr. King. It saved him from some version of the inelegant and tawdry spectacles that have dogged others of his circle in the years since. Without it, could Dr. King have avoided ultimately yielding to the temptation to retire and make a lucrative franchise of his fame, as his family has? Or what about turning SCLC into a personal money machine, as Jesse Jackson did PUSH? This is not to mention the chickens of his sexual transgressions coming home to roost; how much longer would Coretta have put up with them? Nor the embarrassment of his plagiarized doctoral dissertation. The years since 1968 have not been kind to heroes; Dr. King was lucky to escape them.

At the time–and even yet– my discovery of the movement's shadow side was sometimes painful, but only made me marvel the more: "We carry this treasure in earthen vessels," the Apostle Paul wrote to the Corinthians – in a verse not then familiar to me, but which applied to the movement in spades. Somehow, *this* motley crew, this collection of preachers, posers, misfits, rogues and greenhorns, was actually moving history; or at least, moving with That Which moved it. Within this misshapen earthen vessel, there was still an undoubted treasure. Here was a mystery indeed, unrolling right before my eyes, beginning among other things the long-term subversion of my vaunted agnosticism.

IV

Within a day or two, I had made a nervous foray into a downtown farm supply store, where the white clerks and I eyed each other warily, and acquired the movement uniform of overalls and Levi's jacket. Soon someone passed on a small black yarmulke, and I was fully dressed for work.

For the first few nights, I stayed in a house rented by SNCC, sleeping on the top bunk in a small, crowded bedroom. But the atmosphere there was tense: SNCC had been working in Selma since 1962, and some of their staff had paid heavy dues of beatings and jail time. The fact that Dr. King was now sweeping grandly into town and getting more publicity in a day than SNCC had in three years didn't sit well with them. Further, the black nationalist currents already running deep and strong in SNCC made their staff welcome to a white Yankee rookie who was working for their principle rival a muted one, to say the least.

A few days later I was much relieved when a local woman, Mrs. Amelia Platts Boynton, offered to rent me a room in her house on Lapsley Street for $25 per month. Mrs. Boynton was a prominent and assertive woman, both respected and somewhat notorious in Selma's black community. She ran a small insurance office downtown, directly across the street from City Hall and the police station. SCLC set up an office in a corner of the small room, and I was supposed to use her old typewriter to write my dispatches to Atlanta.

But there wasn't much real action to report just yet. For the first two weeks of January, mass meetings were held almost every night. During the daytime, the staff fanned out across Selma's black neighborhoods, canvassing and holding meetings, mobilizing the population for demonstrations. I often tagged along with James Orange as he canvassed and led neighborhood meetings, and was regular at the mass meetings. I found even my white-fly-on-the-wall status very full, even overwhelming.

The canvassing and neighborhood work produced a first big march on Monday January 18. It moved from Brown Chapel downtown to the courthouse, where the county Board of Registrars was holding its twice-monthly voter registration session. Wilson Baker and his city police were in charge that day, and the demonstration went quietly, without arrests or violence.

Baker was a problem for the SCLC staff; he was clearly working the Laurie Pritchett strategy which had stifled the movement in Albany, Georgia. The decision was made to hold another march the next day, and push the envelope.

Tuesday morning the staff asked for fifty volunteers ready to face arrest, and I raised a trembling hand. When we got to the courthouse, it was ringed by a cordon of possemen with hard hats and long billy clubs. Sheriff Jim Clark was there, keeping Baker's police at a distance. We were soon arrested, charged with "failing to leave the place of an unlawful assembly after being warned to disperse by a public officer."

We were put on a bus and taken, I think, to Camp Selma, a prison work camp some miles out of town. When we stepped off the bus, I was cut out of the group and taken inside, to a small room that was painted all white and had a chair and a narrow bed. I was told to wait, and the door was locked.

I sat there for several hours. At first I was rigid with fear, remembering stories about civil rights workers being singled out and beaten in such isolation. But nothing happened, and finally I dozed off, until the guards returned and took me back to the bus, the other marchers, and the safety of black Selma.

This was my first, relatively uneventful arrest. The second, on February 1, has already been described. The third, which came soon after, was a very different, and eye-opening experience.

Before that, though, came a return to Mrs. Boynton's insurance office and the question of those daily dispatches. Now there was definitely something to report, and I made a stab at it.

But almost as soon as my fingers touched the keyboard, they felt weak, almost paralyzed. This was not physical, it was something else; existential is the best word I can find for it. The writing – even the most straightforward declarative sentences laying out the bare journalistic bones of who, what, where, when and why – felt utterly inadequate, and more than that, false and irrelevant. What I was seeing, and taking part in, was infinitely richer, more complex and more ambiguous than the journalistic format could possibly begin to encompass.

What was the trouble, I asked myself? This stuff was not hard:

Five Ws and the H, right? Five or six paragraphs; no problem, right?

But it wasn't a matter of ability. Looking at the few sentences on the page, there seemed to be something grossly pretentious, absurdly arrogant about them, about my very attempt to reduce the richly teeming, tensely kaleidoscopic reality outside Mrs. Boynton's small office to the presumptuous flatness of a reporter's prose. It implied a familiarity with, a mastery of the issues, the locality, and the culture, which I knew I didn't have, yet, if I ever would; not even close.

Quite the contrary – with every passing day it was more intensely obvious just how little I knew about the South, about whites and blacks there, about the political status quo, and how changes in such regimes come about. Not to mention myself and my place in all this.

I didn't, in the end, write more than a couple of these despatches. I hadn't earned the right to. James Orange had told the truth: there were dues yet to pay.

Part of what held me back was a possibly oversensitive reaction to the microcosmic human realities behind the slogans we mouthed and our grand dreams of reshaping southern culture and politics. Yes, something big was happening, and it was a thrill to be on the scene. But what was going on, exactly? Where had it come from, and where was it headed? And how could I be a useful part of it, or at least not an embarrassment?

I didn't have answers to these questions; hell, I hardly knew how to ask them. Again, what came out of my pen that felt honest was not journalistic prose, but a poem, which I wrote down sometime in February:

SELMA STREETS

Here along the Selma streets
Old men like tree stumps,
Young men like defaced pillars,
Whiskers and hair grease and dirty overalls,
Keeping impassive hopeless vigils,

Fraying edges on society's old, but not discarded clothes.

I spring upon them, a dangerous animal,
Dressed in new overalls and enthusiasm,
Hands full of transmigrated dynamite caps:
ONE MAN-ONE VOTE the caps read,
They offer no resistance when I pin the explosives on reluctant lapels,
But then, of course, they never have.
"Come on down to the courthouse, come on come on. . .
Nobody's gonna hurt ya. . . ."
I'm right of course, nobody's ever gonna hurt them anymore, but that's not
> what I'm talking about, not even what I'm thinking. . . .

"Yeah, OK (they don't say Boss Man or Mr. Charlie (thank God?)), sure,
> "Ah'll be downnere inna fewww minuss, sure
>> "Inna fewww minussa, sure
>> "Inna feww, sure
>>> "Suresuresuresuresu""""

Heads nod, graying whiskers flicker in and out of shadow, but the eyes say
> Go away go away, please now just go ahead on away;

The eyes look around me, over, beside, through, but not at, because I don't
> Really exist, can't exist, mustn't exist (I'm thinking about
>> socioeconomic factors, the effects of a political aristocracy,
>>> the philosophy of dynamic nonviolence and, of course, the existential value of
>>>> the local Negro religion, yes, professor, you see, as I explained fully in the
>>>>> footnote on page 47 of my thesis and as we can clearly see

from MacElvain's quite valuable remarks on the subject. . .).

    The walk back up to the listonclay cafe seems longer than when I came down the street, perhaps because the ragged lines of men (Children of what God?)
        The sure, yeah OK men still are standing there,
        New buttons still offending their lapels,
        Eyes still looking, perhaps now a bit more carefully, over, under, around and through,
Then at me when I'm past, but I see them doing it *(go away go away go away)*
Words to an unsung spiritual, prayer of the nonchurchgoers, the Movement of
Those no longer able to move.

Into the cafe, darkness and dirt, filthy flannel figure bending
Across the counter, observing the half-full beer glass as if
It held the answer and maybe it does; I spring again FREEDOM NOW button poised
"Come on down to the courthouse fella, come on come on,
Nobody's gonna hurt ya, whattsa matter, are ya afraid of losing your job–
    (I am of course ready with my arguments to show that one must have courage,
    one must not be afraid to risk everything, one must)?"
But when he turns these eyes upon me (not over, under, around or through)—
    and whispers, says, *"Ain't got no job,"*
And turns back to the more understanding beer glass,
Filthy flannel in the dark and dirt,
Only my mouth continues, throwing up a smokescreen until I can
Get away, away, get away quick, outside and past the
Dying tree stumps, defaced and crumbling pillars,

Glances at the periphery accusing me: you there, boss man,
How do you, O young white man of faith, deal with the substance of things
Hopeless, the evidence of the things that are seen?
But I just walk on in my new overalls, and think of socioeconomics,
And don't say anything.

V

But if I was not to be a flack, what was I to do in Selma to earn my twenty-five dollars a week? Fortunately, I soon found out, at that pay scale Atlanta was not overly intrusive or insistent about productivity and results. And anyway, the need to face up to it was put off for ten days on February 3, when I was arrested for the third time.

This arrest was entirely voluntary, as it turned out. A picket line of mainly high school and college age youth gathered around the Dallas County Courthouse, carrying signs and singing, but quite orderly overall. I watched from across the street, standing near the reporters and cameras, as the possemen stopped them and made them stand there, strung out along the sidewalk.

It seemed likely they would be arrested. There were no other SCLC staffers in the line, and there was no need for me to join them. But then something made me want to, despite, or perhaps because I had just been in jail with Dr. King two days before. And I did, walking quietly across the pavement to take a spot in the line.

It was cold that morning, and we could see our breath. I was warm enough, though, because a few days before, at one of the churches, I had foraged in a large pile of discarded clothing, and come up with an oversized blue wool Air Force greatcoat. It was thick, stiff and ugly, but it did the job.

It also may have saved my manhood. Several of the possemen carried cattle prods. A couple of the prods were almost as long as a man's arm, and their stacked up batteries made for a jolt that reputedly could sear flesh.

Possemen passed up and down our line, telling us to move on, and then making use of their prods. A couple of times one of the small ones snapped and buzzed against my earlobes, making me wince and gasp. Then I repeatedly felt the longer ones poking at my rump, and probing between my legs. But the thick wool of the coat and baggy overalls beneath it combined to protect my vitals. The prongs buzzed against my leg and I caught a whiff of heated wool, but that thankfully was all.

When they had had their fill of trying to fry us, the possemen gave way to sheriff Clark, who angrily ordered us inside, to meet our fate at the bar of County Judge James Hare.

Judge Hare quickly sentenced us to a $50 fine and five days in jail for contempt of court. If we failed to pay the fine, he ordered that we be held for an additional "blank" days at three dollars per day; evidently the math was not his strong point.

But before we were taken away, we were left to sit on the benches of his courtroom for what seemed like hours. Evidently there was legal maneuvering going on behind the scenes, involving the NAACP Legal Defense Fund, county, state and even federal authorities; but none of this was visible to us as time passed and we grew more hungry and restless.

Next to me sat a tall young man, and after awhile he whispered to me that he had to use the bathroom. I urged him to speak up about it, but when he did a deputy gruffly brushed off the request. He groaned and squirmed, while I sweated in my now stifling overcoat.

At length there was stirring in the hallway outside. A deputy stuck his head in the door and said, "Who was it that wanted to use the bathroom?" He looked significantly at my companion. The youth just shook his head now.

"All right then, let's go!" barked the deputy, and the room began to rumble as one by one the rows of students rose and shuffled toward the hall. My seatmate stood up and walked quickly out. Glancing down, I saw that my coat was slopping into a large pool of urine, and leaped up to get away.

We were led out to a schoolbus, which drove to the middle of town where the National Guard Armory stood. The Armory was a large vacant building, whitewashed brick on the outside, with a dirt floor and big garage-type doors at either end. The doors were opened, the bus drove right into it, and we were led off and told to sit down.

There were already dozens of people sitting cross-legged on the packed dirt, and I joined them, being careful to find a spot at least one row back from the front. Sheriff Clark and his deputies were striding back and forth in front of our squatting ranks, and I felt him glowering down at me. Soon he began shouting commands:

"All those who are in junior high school or below, stand up!"

Kids here and there rose, and were led away; I had the impression they were being sent home. Then there was a similar command for high school students. More left, and I was suddenly in the front row. I sat there, feeling the cool of the ground, afraid to look around or behind me, foolishly imagining that I would thereby not draw attention to myself.

Then Clark was walking, no, swaggering in my direction. He pulled up right in front of me, a few feet away. I didn't look up, but I could see his boots, and the end of his big leather holster. I thought I could hear him snickering. Then he spoke, and I was sure he was:

"All non-students, come over here."

"Non-students" in that setting was a code for "outside agitators." I had not seen any other movement staffers in the line or the courthouse, so as far as I knew, I was the only one who fit his description. This meant I was headed for some solitary trip to – where? The Alabama River that swirled darkly below its high banks along the edge of town? It was less than a mile away.

I didn't stand up immediately. My stomach suddenly felt very hollow, and I knew my knees were shaking.

What happened next was that those few seconds of hesitation seemed to expand into a long, almost indefinite span; or better, for a brief interval I seemed to slip out of the normal stream of time. I sat there, and an eerie sense of the nearness of death came over me like a cold breeze. This was not the normal fear I had felt often enough in Selma. It was something more existential, something reminiscent of The Absurd or the Nothingness I had read about in Camus and Sartre in college philosophy classes.

Sheriff Clark was the herald of this gray blankness, but he was not its embodiment. It was a much more impersonal presence, something that always hovered nearby but which usually was not noticed. Like a hole into which the unwary might stumble and fall unawares. I had the sense, without becoming hysterical or maudlin, that when I stood up I might well be taking the last few steps in my life's path. I felt more resigned than anything else.

I stood up.

Clark pointed to a bus waiting nearby. It was empty, and the open door was a dark grasping rectangular hole. I climbed slowly in and sat down on a middle bench seat, limp in the hands of a blind fate.

Then to my shock and relief, others began climbing on to the bus: ten, a dozen, twenty. As they quietly came up the aisle, the sense of being beyond time receded; I slipped back into the stream of events. I also deduced, correctly, that if Clark and his men had harbored homicidal fantasies about me, they would have to put them in abeyance in the presence of all these others; too many witnesses.

After a short jerky ride, existentialist nightmares resolved themselves into the familiar shape of City Hall. A few moments later, my fellow passengers and I were back up in the big dayroom on the third floor which I had shared briefly with Dr. King.

VII

There were two distinct phases to this stretch of imprisonment The first began with about a dozen of us in the dayroom, among whom I was the only white and the sole civil rights worker. I was also, I soon figured, the oldest in the group. Most of the rest were students at Selma University.

Selma U. was a tiny church-run black junior college and Bible school which occupied a few acres on Lapsley St. several blocks from my digs with Mrs. Boynton. I had visited the campus a couple of times, and was suitably shocked by the rudimentary character of the library. The librarian, a stiff-looking gray-haired woman, gently but firmly turned away the offer of a few volumes from my own collection; her thin, frosty smile made clear that they did not feel a need to be patronized by the likes of me, thank you very much.

In the jail dayroom, once the students and I collected ourselves, we surveyed our domain. In the absence of Monday's crowd, it was bleak: several mattresses had been brought in and left on the floor; the steel tables were bare, and the toilet gaped in the corner. The regular prisoners, again confined to their cells, looking on impassively

To keep our spirits up, we formed a circle and sang freedom songs for awhile. Our voices were answered by a chorus from the women's side; neither group was as loud as I remembered from two days before, but then neither group was anywhere near as big.

Singing, it turned out, was the main thing we were able to do with any semblance of discipline or solidarity. Our problems began to surface when supper was brought in, some hours later. We were, of course, ravenous.

Since Dr. King was not here, there was no temptation for the authorities to indulge us. Nor, for that matter, were we enjoying the hospitality of the relatively moderate Wilson Baker. Thus Sheriff Clark's menu was drastically simpler than my feast at Dr. King's expense: our rations consisted of somewhat less than a cup of mushy blackeye peas apiece, accompanied by a two-inch square of dry corn bread. This, water, and all the salt we wanted, made up the entire menu. Hungry as we were, we were repelled by this meager meal, and there was much complaining, even as we ate it

Then we were left to face the main ingredient of jail fare, which is boredom. As night finally settled in, we drifted off to various of the bare mattresses, and struggled for sleep in the lonely, tinny darkness.

The second day, when it became clear that the breakfast menu was actually a brunch, featuring the same elements as dinner, our morale began to suffer. More candidly, it sank fast.

This funk was not improved when several new prisoners joined us. A few of these were protesters, but a couple others loudly insisted that they had simply been swept up off the sidewalk while minding their own business. One among these spent much of several hours pounding on the bars of the door, and the adjoining steel panels, demanding to be released, and shouting warnings of what his momma was going to do to the deputies when she came to get him.

Several others talked less loudly but with equal insistence about the injustice of it all, and the havoc their mommas would wreak in turn when they rode to the rescue. I never heard any of them mention a father as a figure to be reckoned with, or even taken note of.

Besides the grumbling directed at the guards, squabbles soon broke out between the Selma U. students and others, particularly a young fellow from rural Dallas County. This youth, who was soon christened "Cool," by the others, had evidently been something of a dandy in his rural school society. His clothes had a studied appearance, if a rustic one. This and his carriage evoked disdainful snickers and then audible jeers from the townies. Cool was a good-natured sort, however, and was slow to rise to the bait. He reminded the townies that we were supposed to be in this together, as part of a common struggle for advancement.

I took this as a cue to attempt to exert some sort of organizer's influence. To divert their attention from this fractiousness, I talked about the common enemy, Sheriff Clark, and especially his starvation diet. If we stood together, I urged, maybe we could force him to change it, and come through with some real food.

This seemed to rally the troops, and before long, after a round of freedom songs, they had all agreed to a brief statement I scribbled on a scrap of paper found in my overalls pocket. It announced a hunger strike, in protest of the corn bread-blackeye peas regimen and demanded something better.

This felt good; as I shoved it through the meal slot I had brief fantasies of being the ringleader of a tough, united band of activists, taking on the brutal sheriff with our bare hands. Just the story, I figured, would sound good to my SCLC peers when I got out.

But Clark seemed to know my comrades better than I did. By late afternoon, as the smell of blackeye peas again began to drift into the dayroom, I was shocked to hear talk of desertion among the troops. Several of the guys soon admitted as much: they didn't like the food, but dammit, they were hungry.

When the trays were passed in, some of us refused them, but half the guys took them, ignoring my pleas with a guilty kind of bravado. Our hunger strike, it appeared, was strictly a between-meals affair.

Thus humbled, I passed much of the next two days stretched out by myself on a mattress. I had noticed that the talk altered when I sat in on the others' bull sessions, and there was no way to overcome my handicaps of being white and from out of town. But my choice of solitude was not a matter of moping or pouting. Instead I faced away from the others on my mattress, pretending to doze or daydream, while actually listening carefully. This eavesdropping, or as it might be called, field work, became very interesting, as I set out to learn what the Selma U. students talked about when they thought they were alone.

This observation paid off. While they spoke of many things at one time or another, the boys were preoccupied above all with sex, and specifically an ongoing campaign of seduction aimed at various coeds at their school. Besides boasting of their conquests, they spent much time assembling coalitions and laying out strategies aimed at steering one or another girl into the bed of a pre-selected male.

To hear them talk, these young men were highly accomplished at such joint efforts, and their recounting of past conquests and eager anticipation of future achievements made for astonishing listening. As a young adult male, I had thought of myself as pretty pre-occupied with sex. But my level of horniness was small potatoes compared to that being rehearsed only a few feet away.

As the days unrolled and I kept listening, it came to me that these young men were bent, however unwittingly, on acting out and fulfilling the stereotype of the black male as feral sexual predator. It also seemed evident that the pattern of competitive sexual conquests among their female peers was somehow related to their dependence on mother figures; but I couldn't figure out exactly how.

One conclusion I did reach during these days of listening and reflection was that southern racism –maybe all white racism–was like a three-legged stool, standing on the pillars of money, sex and religion. Black labor was exploited for the profit of white overlords; the men were infantilized, the women both built up and abused; and the Bible was somehow made to justify it all. No one of these was central, but none could be entirely disentangled from the other either. For what it's worth, I still think that's the case.

About four days into our stay, one of the group who said he had been swept up by the police fell ill. It seemed to be some kind of intestinal complaint, and he sweated and moaned in apparent agony, calling for his mother and for the deputies to let him out. By that night he was screaming, and the rest of us took up his cause, pounding on the walls, shouting for his momma and demanding a doctor.

Finally, after what seemed like hours, a deputy opened the door wide enough to peek in briefly, then beat a hasty retreat. A few moments later a squad of them appeared bearing a stretcher, and the victim was carried out, still moaning.

Watching him go, we all felt a renewal of righteous anger and solidarity. What were they doing—leaving us in here to sicken and die, unknown and unmourned? After another lusty round of freedom songs, I sensed it was time to step forward again. Were we going to put up with such treatment, I demanded? Hell, no! And if not, how could we express our outrage over such treatment of the sick, and the continuing unfair treatment of us all, particularly the lousy food.

This time I let them make the suggestion: a hunger strike. I reminded them that this was a drastic step, which would mean short-term suffering, and which could end up making us look twice foolish. But they insisted, and I again wrote up a short list of demands and stuffed it through the food slot.

There was no official response to this second manifesto either, and by late the next morning, when the blackeye peas arrived again, this boycott suffered the same fate as the first.

Did the deputies survey the empty trays and laugh at us? They had every right; as resisters, we were miserable. By now, however, I was more jaded myself, and felt less humiliation. Besides, I had worries of my own: the isolation and lack of communication from outside was getting to me: what, I worried, if something happened to Tish, a car wreck, a robbery? I was safe enough, so far, but the world outside was big and dangerous, and what was going on there was, for us, a menacing blank.

These questions hung over me, unanswered; but soon there were distractions. First, Sunday came, and with it a break in the feeding routine: in place of blackeye peas, the food trays brought us soggily fried chicken wings, which we all greedily attacked.

Just as welcome, especially to me, this was soon followed by a new influx of prisoners, from renewed protest marches downtown. They were mostly older, and included a few whites as well. Among them was James Bevel, whose electric presence brought me to an unaccustomed state of alertness.

Everyone else knew of Bevel too, but when we looked to him for a sermon or a round of freedom singing, he gave us something else: finding a broom in the corner, he began furiously sweeping the littered floor of the day room, and explaining to the group some of what I had heard Dr. King tell the trusty, about Gandhi's insistence on making prison time an edifying, uplifting experience. That couldn't be achieved, he scolded us, in a compound that looked like a pigsty.

Before the newcomers got settled in, however, the county decided to deal with the crowd by farming it out. Bars clanged, deputies shouted, and soon enough many of us were on the buses again, headed out of town. Bevel never got to move on to the next lesson after cleanliness; too bad for us.

We didn't go far, however, before turning into a gravel road. I glimpsed a sign by the brushy roadside; it read, "Camp Selma." Our new home.

VII

Camp Selma was presumably used to house the chain gang prisoners who worked on the area's roads. It consisted, as near as we could tell, of several barracks-like shelters. The one I was taken to was a long rectangular room. It had a flat grey concrete floor, and was completely empty except for a seatless toilet in one corner and a tub of water with a black enameled dipper in another. Instead of windows, there were screened openings all along one wall. Clearly the keepers of the camp were more concerned about ventilation during the long, punishing Alabama summers than with the February chill that now streamed in.

Walking the fifty feet or so to the other end of the bay, I peered through the screens. Outside the day was grey; drops of mist glistened on dry leaves, and a few chickens were strutting and perching on some odd metal fixtures scattered about the grass.

Wait a minute – looking again, I realized the metal fixtures were not odd, but simply out of context: they were metal bedframes, dozens of them. The frames were not rusty, so they had not been there long.

Then it was obvious: the cots had been here, inside the bays, probably until this morning. They had been moved outside on our account. The mattresses were stowed somewhere else, presumably away from the damp.

Most of the youths I had shared the county day room with were herded to some other wing; here I found myself with a new batch of compatriots, all older men. As more of them followed me to the screens and understood what had been done, there were cries of anger and outrage. Wasn't this worse than a concentration camp? The Nazis at least provided cots (or so we had seen in the movies).

But there was no help for it. Who was there to complain to? Who even knew where we were? We sang, milled around, and then slumped to the cold floor in ones and twos.

As our condition sank in, I was soon revealed as one of the wealthiest among us. My riches consisted of my heavy Air Force overcoat. Unfashionable, even gauche on the outside, here it was the acme of comfort. Already it had saved my testicles from the possemen's cattle prods at the court house; now it became unquestionably the softest, warmest item of bedding in the place.

We were kept in this bay for five more days. Among the other inmates were a pudgy local preacher, who gave us blustery daily sermons and repeatedly sneaked onto my "bed" for uninvited naps. there was also a quietly militant SNCC worker, and two Unitarian ministers from Boston.

Many SNCC staffers normally held themselves aloof from the likes of me, a white kid working for "De Lawd"; but under these circumstances he deigned to talk a bit. He also shared with me a thin tabloid newspaper which he had evidently smuggled in under his overalls. I was amazed to find it was the *National Guardian*, a Marxist weekly from New York. In it were long articles about the "people's struggle" in Alabama, and a long report about "revolutionary" Vietnam.

I don't think I had ever seen a piece of real American Marxist literature up close before; in my 1950s military family, I had absorbed anti-communist sentiments with my daily cereal. But there's no denying that subversive propaganda gains in plausibility and appeal when approached behind the Establishment's bars, and I read the *Guardian* with great interest.

The Vietnam article was by an Australian, Wilfred Burchett, who was evidently a veteran reporter; that is, while he had a clear leftist point of view, the piece was plausible and journalistic. Its general drift was that the liberation forces were advancing, but that the American imperialists were also escalating their invasion and bombing attacks.

(And indeed they were. During this same week, Dr. King had gone to Washington, planning to see White House officials about a voting rights bill. But his meetings had been abruptly canceled, as President Johnson huddled with his advisors, making the operational decisions which would decisively increase U.S. involvement in the war: more troops, more bombing, more fervid talk about American "honor.")

We did not know about this, of course; and in truth, I had not thought much, if at all about Vietnam before now. But as the Guardian moved from hand to hand around our bay, Vietnam seeped into our consciousness anyway, where it soon became lodged like a kidney stone, not to be passed for many years.

The *Guardian*'s impact was reinforced by my conversations with the two Unitarians, Gordon Gibson and Ira Blalock. I was interested in talking to them anyway, as my visits to the Unitarian congregation in Atlanta had left me, among other things, wondering about attending one of their seminaries. We were soon taking lengthy "walks," pacing up and down the middle of the bay, and talking about a wide range of things, personal, religious and political.

When I asked one of them what he preached in his church back home, he grinned and replied, "Socialism." Then he produced, from an inside pocket, two copies of the *Monthly Review*, a scholarly Marxist periodical.

So there it was again. I spent more hours reading these journals from cover to cover, becoming familiar with Paul Baran and Paul Sweezy, its editors and principal contributors, and struggling with notions like the tendency of surplus to rise, and realizing that I was probably destined to be part of the petit bourgeoisie.

This reading and the talk did not immediately convert me to Marxism, but it launched me into a period of interest in and study of the *Monthly Review* brand of it which was to last several years.

Right away, I learned that in this field, even terminology was loaded and hazardous. Baran and Sweezy, for instance, called themselves Marxian, rather than Marxist or Communist; and it seemed evident that they were attempting to steer an independent course in an ideological channel full of sectarian shoals as well as the mines of official repression.

Someone else, perhaps one of the ministers, also had a couple of paperbacks, one with several plays by Sartre, and another by Camus, *The Rebel*, I believe. So besides Marxism (or perhaps "Marxianism"), the sojourn in Camp Selma also introduced me to European existentialism.

Sartre I could follow, at least somewhat. I read his play "No Exit" which placed its characters in "Hell," which turned out to be, not a place of fire and brimstone, but a drawing room in which one was trapped with others: "Hell is other people," as its most famous line put it. I also thought I got the drift of another play, "Dirty Hands," which was that if you were going to act meaningfully in the world, you would end up doing evil of necessity; idealism was doomed, and probably only a bourgeois illusion at that.

Camus was tougher going. His celebrated essay seemed to be built on the question, "Why live?" put rather more bluntly in the form of the query, "Why not commit suicide?" This formulation seemed too gloomy to me; I had never contemplated suicide, and didn't think I ever would.

Despite this reaction, I had the feeling my sympathies would lie more with Camus both politically and humanistically, than to Sartre; I gathered that Camus had broken with Sartre over the questions of supporting terrorism and the Communist Party. After all, under Dr. King's tutelage, I was supposed to be learning how to be a nonviolent activist. Nevertheless, I found Sartre easier to read, and never finished *The Rebel*.

Talking with the Unitarians about these grand issues of philosophy and politics helped pass the time during our miles of walks up and down the length of the bay; but nothing intellectual could compare with the more worldly, immediate issue of food. After the hated blackeye peas in town, I now found I had not sufficiently appreciated the wonders of beans.

Navy beans in particular, big white ones. At Camp Selma we were still served only twice a day; but the servings were larger, the corn bread thicker and fresher, and the beans tastier. It also made our bay more fragrant, and at night, more noisy. But these were minor drawbacks. On reflection, this menu, simple enough in its own way, made some sense: regular prisoners, men working on road gangs all day, needed more substantial nutrition than the wretches who were simply sitting in their cells downtown.

And then one night, to our great surprise, we were trooped into the Spartan dining room to find a tall, portly figure waiting for us. It was the Rev. C.C. Brown, a local black preacher, and behind him on a long table were several large trays, heaped with steaming mounds of fried chicken.

I had heard of Rev. Brown, but was not acquainted with him. He had not been among the parade of local preachers taking their brief turns in the pulpit at Brown Chapel as warmups for Dr. King and his circle. When his name had come up in staff meetings, he was dismissed as an "Uncle Tom," a marginal black minister who kowtowed to powerful local whites in pursuit of his own interests.

I didn't learn the details until later, but Brown's position, like that of most real people, was more complicated than the stereotype laid on him. It turned out that Brown's mother had been white, from a prominent local family. She had married a black man, and then refused to accept banishment from the area as the price of her transgression. She was, however, forced to become de facto "black," for all social purposes.

When she died later that same year, the Selma Times-Journal was thrown into a quandary: They were unable because of her lineage to ignore the event, as they routinely overlooked the deaths of other "colored" residents. But if they ran an obituary, how would they identify her? She was legally married, but when Blacks were mentioned in their columns, they were, by southern custom, not identified as Mrs. or Mr.

The editors attempted to finesse this conundrum by calling her simply "Senior Citizen" Brown.

Her son Claude had grown up in Selma, been educated at church colleges in the north, and become a Presbyterian minister. In 1965 he led a small church on West Jeff Davis Avenue, smack on the invisible line between black and white neighborhoods. He also ran several church schools in Wilcox County, to the south of Selma. In Wilcox, a century after the Civil War's end, there were still no public schools for blacks. Brown's control of the school budgets, buying food and other supplies for them, gave him some weight with Selma's merchants and bankers; and his family background gave him other contacts, since many prominent whites were his blood kin.

It was these connections he had called on to get into Camp Selma for a fried chicken mission of mercy. I heard no snide murmuring about "Uncle Tom" that night, as all of us crowded hungrily around to wolf it down. Finger-licking good, indeed.

Other than being introduced to existentialism, Marxism, and Vietnam – not small matters, after all– the stay at Camp Selma was uneventful. My new Unitarian comrades and I walked and talked our way through hundreds of laps up and down the center of the bay. Each night I groaned with the others at the hardness of the concrete floor, but was thankful for the clumsy thickness of my Air Force coat; during the day I regularly shooed other prisoners away from it. Outside, the grass seen through our screens was pale but appealingly green; the empty bedframes began to rust. After Rev. Brown's chicken feast, we returned to beans, which were still better than blackeye peas.

Finally, after five days, a guard came to the door of the bay, unlocked it and led us out, back to the buses. We were driven into town, glad to be presumably on our way to freedom, but still unclear about why we had been released. Not having paid my $50 fine, the "blank" days at three dollars per day to which Judge Hare had sentenced me still had several more to run. Our release had something to do with the removal of our cases to federal court, but to this day I'm unsure exactly how we were sprung.

No question about it, though: I preferred freedom to confinement; that was the last time I went to jail in Selma.

Chapter Five
The Selma-Montgomery March

I

Once back in circulation, I caught up quickly: Tish, it turned out, was safe; my jailhouse fears were just that. She had even made plans to come to Selma, telling her Atlanta employers that her father, who lived in Denver, had fallen deathly ill and she had to rush to his side. Once she was in Selma, she too became determined to stay; so she called her boss and, telling him her father had now died, quit. We soon made a furtive trip back to Atlanta to pack and move. All our worldly belongings – oh, the simplicity of youth – fit into a Volkswagen bus borrowed for the journey.

Tish was put to work typing and answering the phone for SCLC in Mrs. Boynton's insurance office across from City Hall. Before long, she was added to the payroll, at a blatantly discriminatory $15 per week, a total of $40 for our fledgling household.

And I – what of my botched assignment as a local correspondent for headquarters?

Fortunately, when I re-emerged after ten days in stir, it seemed to be forgotten. This was lucky on a couple of counts: principally because I still was unable to write anything in prose about what was happening; but also because the movement was heating up.

The push and pull between Wilson Baker and Sheriff Clark had continued nonstop while I was in jail. For much of the time Baker was in command, and his kid-glove treatment was working: the turnout for marches had dwindled. Then Clark had singlehandedly revived the movement on February 10, when he corralled two hundred students from a picket line outside the courthouse and drove them like terrified cattle, screaming and gasping, at a run along the river several miles out of town, with reporters following. This forced-march humiliated Baker, and produced howls of outrage in the black community. It also re-filled the mass meetings, and on February 15 produced the largest march Selma had yet seen.

Although there was, indeed, much to write about in these days, in this tense atmosphere, reporters were in plentiful supply to do it for me, and there were other things I could do which seemed useful.

One of these became my main achievement as an agitator, when I visited my Selma University jail buddies on their small campus. They were restive under their president, who was firmly of the Booker T. Washington persuasion, that blacks should get education and keep out of trouble. After a noisy confrontation with the president during their chapel assembly, I helped them lead a student exodus from the campus to join a march to the courthouse.

James Orange and the other SCLC staffers in town were amazed: "Chuck done *turned out* Selma U," was the comment, and they began showing me a bit more respect. This was gratifying, of course, but the memory of our failed hunger strikes in jail left me under no illusions that this foray made me any kind of charismatic activist.

In any event, the Selma University achievement was quickly lost in the enlarging whirl of events. Within a week, the focus of attention shifted from Selma to Marion, a smaller town half an hour northeast, where marches by local blacks had been met with a much more violent response. In Marion on the night of February 18, Jimmie Lee Jackson was shot in the stomach by a state trooper when Jackson went to the aid of his aged father, who was being beaten.

Reaction to the Marion attack was strong and nationwide. The Alabama authorities did their part to keep this indignation at white heat, first by pushing a resolution through the state senate supporting the state troopers' repression in Marion. Then the troopers' commander, Col. Al. Lingo, served Jackson in his hospital bed with a warrant charging him with assault and battery with intent to murder one of his men.

II

Late the next Thursday night, with Jimmie Lee Jackson still fighting for his life in the hospital, James Bevel suddenly burst into the single room I shared with Tish in Mrs. Boynton's house. He flipped on the light, startling us awake, and began talking rapidly, as if resuming a conversation that had been going on only a few moments before.

Blinking in the abrupt brightness, we heard him say that the next step for the movement had to be a march, not to the courthouse downtown, or in Marion, but rather from Selma all the way to Montgomery, fifty miles down Highway 80 through Lowndes County.

It was, on the face of it, a frightening plan: Lowndes County was known as a place where violence against would-be black voters and their advocates was swift and terrible. The county population was three-fourths black, yet not a single person of color was registered to vote there. Lowndes was also almost completely rural: Hayneville, the county seat, was a mere hamlet, and the main road, US Highway 80, wound its way through long stretches of swamp, with thick growths of trees and bushes on both sides, providing perfect cover for potential bushwhackers.

Bevel acknowledged the hazards, but moved quickly past them to focus on the logic of his plan, which was clear: Jackson had been attacked by state troopers, who were run from Montgomery. The racist voting regulations were also made there, by the legislature. The governor spewed vitriol about "agitators" from his office in the white capitol. And with the public attention now focused on Alabama, any attacks on a march would only increase the pressure for change.

All this, Bevel insisted, made Montgomery the most legitimate target for a serious effort to petition the government for redress of grievances. And it was time.

In a few minutes, having won our approval of the idea, Bevel just as abruptly hurried out into the night.

This whole episode was exciting and puzzling; I was not used to being consulted on matters of high strategy, and certainly not at such an hour. But it turned out that Tish and I were only two of many: it was part of Bevel's style to try out such ideas on various people, to test the waters, refine the plan, and figure out how best to present it.

The time for such a presentation soon came: The next morning, February 26, Jimmie Lee Jackson died.

That day was the turning point of the Selma campaign. Whatever reluctance was felt by Dr. King and others about Bevel's audacious plan was swept away by the reaction to Jackson's death. Against this background, when Bevel stepped into the pulpit of the little Marion church for Jackson's funeral on February 28, his eloquence was enriched by anger. His repeated calls, building on a line from the Book of Esther, 4:4, that "I must go see the king," and that "We must go to Montgomery and see the king," were all but irresistible.

Later that same day, Dr. King announced that yes, there would be a march to Montgomery, beginning one week later, Sunday, March seventh.

III

Bevel's sense of timing proved to be uncanny. More than once in his brilliant sermons, he had told us that he, like many other black people in the South, might be light on formal education, but that he was an expert in one subject above all: "I *study* my white folks. I *know* 'em."

This finely-honed intuition, based on lifelong observation, rightly told him that the tensions among white leaders and their more dangerous followers were moving steadily toward some kind of climax, and the Montgomery march plan would jack up the intensity by several notches.

Once it became clear there would in fact be an attempt to march to Montgomery, it was also obvious that Governor Wallace could not allow it to happen. His administration, indeed the whole state, was taking a tremendous public beating in the wake of Jimmie Lee Jackson's death. Wallace could not afford to see its reputation further sullied by more bloodshed.

But Wallace was in something of a box, because he also knew his state troopers could not be relied on to deal with the pilgrimage peaceably. Their commander, Col. Al Lingo, was maneuvering secretly with Jim Clark to set up a confrontation with the marchers that both men had long been itching for. They wanted it to happen outside the Selma city limits, where that pusillanimous Wilson Baker could not interfere. The two men's more violent white supremacist camp followers caught the scent of impending attack, and began migrating toward the city to join in.

At Brown Chapel, we smelled trouble too, and it made our preparations for the march somewhat half-hearted. We didn't do much in the way of serious logistical planning for a fifty-mile trek by several hundred people. That's because few of us figured the march would get very far; we all expected to be arrested before we got out of town. Actually, we *hoped* to get arrested before we went past the bridge; better the county jail or Camp Selma, where the walls kept terrorists out, than the ominous grey terrain of those swamps, where dozens or hundreds could easily be hidden.

These apprehensions were reinforced on Saturday, March 6, when a small group of progressive white Alabamians, gathered to show support for the movement, was attacked by other whites near the courthouse, and Baker's police narrowly averted a full-scale riot. We didn't know whether to be relieved or more afraid when we heard, later that same day, that Wallace had issued a proclamation forbidding the Montgomery march, as "not conducive" to traffic and commerce in the state.

Actually, the prospects for violence were increasing hourly. Wallace had, in his way, done his best: he had ordered his troopers to disperse the march peacefully, once it crossed the Edmund Pettus Bridge over the Alabama River. Jim Clark had been lured out of town for a weekend talk show appearance in Washington. With Wilson Baker also taking a few days off, Selma Mayor Joe Smitherman had pledged full cooperation with the governor's plan.

But Smitherman was a rookie. Baker, the veteran, sensed that real trouble was coming, and on his return he told the mayor he did not want his men taking part in the bridge action. Baker proposed instead that he arrest the entire march right after it left the church, thus keeping them out of the troopers' clutches entirely. When Smitherman insisted that he had confidence in the governor's pledge of peaceful dispersal, Baker threatened to resign on the spot, and only relented when Smitherman agreed to sharply limit the police presence at the bridge.

We didn't know about this confrontation then, or at least I didn't. But as Sunday morning came and we gathered at Brown Chapel, the prospect of violence hung in the air like a fog. Homemade bedrolls were piled near the platform, and we listened to instructions on how to deal with tear gas, which we heard had been issued to the troopers.

Our expectation was that the march would proceed in two or three waves, one following another as the marchers were arrested. As the final round of singing and pep talks were being made in the church, the staff gathered in the parsonage next door, to get our own marching orders.

There were too many of us for the living room furniture, so most, including me, sat cross-legged on the floor. Dr. King had said he would lead the march, but he wasn't there. This was another sign of the prospect of trouble: After the episode of the night march, I knew Dr. King was not afraid for himself; but I also knew that his inner circle was afraid for him, and protected him as best they could. They had, I figured, somehow kept him away.

In his absence, Andrew Young gave out our instructions. He went around the circle, assigning this one to the first wave, that one to the second. Finally he got to me.

I looked up at him, trying, I am sure without success, to mask my fear. The sensation was not so different from what had come over me when I sat in the field house staring at Jim Clark's boots. Yet the sense of being a footsoldier in an army was once again clear: fear before battle was not shameful, and despite it I would carry out my orders then, as I had been ready to do for the planned night march, and as I had on those other marches.

But Andy was merciful. Gazing down at me, he murmured something about my needing to deal with the press, and assigned me to the second wave. As he moved on I tried, probably with no more success, to disguise my relief.

Andy, Bevel and Hosea Williams flipped coins to see who would lead the first wave, and Hosea lost.

In a few moments we were back in the church, where Hosea, looking very solemn indeed, led the crowd in a round of "God Will

Take Care of You." Then, bedrolls hoisted, and with John Lewis of SNCC beside Hosea, the marchers moved out of the church, and down Sylvan Street.

IV

Wilson Baker had been told that Col. Al Lingo would meet Jim Clark in Montgomery on his return from Washington, and keep him busy there until the march was over. Instead, Clark and Lingo arrived at the Pettus Bridge just in time to urge the troopers and Clark's possemen, many of these on horseback, onto the attack.

The marchers were beaten and tear-gassed, then chased back across the bridge and through downtown Selma. Troopers and possemen pursued them all the way to the Carver projects surrounding Brown Chapel. Baker tried to stop Clark once he got near Sylvan Street, but the sheriff elbowed angrily past him and the melee continued unabated. Baker ordered his police out of the area, to prevent them from taking any further part in the violence.

I watched the initial assault on the march from the bluff across the river, where I had ridden with someone who had a car. As the cries of the marchers moved back across the bridge, the mist of tear gas drifted our way, bright white in the midday sunlight. We drove off, taking back streets to Good Samaritan Hospital, a small facility in the black neighborhood run by Catholic missionaries. Looking in briefly, we saw the emergency staff, wide-eyed and grave, coping with chaos, as hysterical marchers streamed in, rubbing their eyes, crying, bleeding, and limping.

At the church, we figured the second wave would presumably be getting ready, and it would soon be my turn. Heading back, I was grim but resolved, and also a bit ashamed at having been spared; after this, I would be ready to face whatever they were dishing out.

At Brown Chapel, though, there was only more chaos: People rushed up and down the steps, some yelling defiance, throwing bottles and rocks, and vowing to get their guns and retaliate. Seeing troopers and possemen still circling the church, it was obvious that heading off further escalation was the most immediate need, so I joined a few others who went from one end of the steps to another, pleading for everyone to go inside, pushing them toward the doors.

Finally most of the people were inside, and I followed them. The church was full of acrid fumes, evaporating from the marcher's clothes and skin, and I was soon coughing with the rest. But before long Hosea Williams mounted the podium, his face dripping where he had rinsed off the tear gas. His denunciation of the brutality was in full throat, and helped refocus the crowd's attention away from outside.

Hosea was soon joined by John Lewis, whose skull had been fractured by the trooper's clubs, but who refused treatment until he had added his voice to Hosea's. Significantly, his message was that it was unconscionable that Lyndon Johnson would be sending U.S. troops to Vietnam in the purportedFebruary 7, 2005 defense of freedom, and not be sending them as well to Alabama to defend us. We roared our outraged agreement.

Soon there was another staff meeting at the parsonage. Again seated on the floor, most of us were spectators to a heated telephone conference, in which Hosea, Andy, and others debated loudly with each other and Dr. King, somewhere on the other end, about what to do next.

We quickly figured out that there would be no immediate second wave. Instead, the question was now whether to march again the next day, Monday, or wait until Tuesday and in the meantime try to mobilize supporters from around the nation to join us. Those on the phone, once their shouting died down, finally agreed that Tuesday was the day.

V

[The next day, far from the chaos of Selma, the U.S. Supreme Court issued a little-noticed decision in the case of U.S. v. Seeger.

Daniel A. Seeger was a New Yorker who had become a pacifist and an agnostic in college. When he applied to his draft board for conscientious objector status, his claim was denied on the basis that Seeger's pacifism was not based, as the law then stated, on "religious training and belief," which had been amplified to involve "an individual's belief in a relation to a

Supreme Being. . . . "

Seeger claimed his agnostic beliefs were as authentically religious as those of any theist. He was tried and convicted of refusing to submit to induction into the military. He appealed.

The Supreme Court agreed with Seeger, concluding that the actual meaning of the law's phrase "religious training and belief" was "whether it is a sincere and meaningful belief occupying in the life of its possessor a place parallel to that filled by the God of those admittedly qualified for the exemption." It unanimously reversed Seeger's conviction.

Remarkable as the decision was, Justice William O. Douglas filed a concurring opinion which was even more adventurous. Looking beyond the narrow issues in the case, he noted that "The words 'a supreme Being' have no narrow technical meaning in the field of religion. Long before the birth of our Judeo-Christian civilization the idea of God had taken hold in many forms." He added that "When the present Act was adopted in 1948 we were a nation of Buddhists, Confucianists, and Taoists, as well as Christians." Citing eminent authorities, he pointed out that "if 'God' is taken to mean a personal Creator of the universe, then the Buddhist has no interest in the concept."

Among the few who noticed this decision were the small staff of the Central Committee for Conscientious Objectors in Philadelphia, or CCCO. They published a Handbook for Conscientious Objectors which had already been through six editions to keep up with legal developments in its narrow field of interest. The staff immediately set about updating the seventh edition, which appeared the next month.

At the time I knew nothing of either the decision or the CCCO, and almost nothing of the issues involved. But this decision would affect my life as much as anything else that happened that week.]

VI

On Tuesday, I made sure I marched, close to the front. The atmosphere that morning was quite different from Sunday. On the surface, it appeared that Dr. King was leading us to defy a last-minute federal court order, issued to delay a march until a hearing had been held. Troopers were massed across the bridge, right where they had been on what was already called Bloody Sunday. This should have been ominous, not to say terrifying.

But it wasn't. For one thing, there were hundreds more of us in line, and Dr. King was flanked by numerous religious dignitaries, including the head of the Unitarian church and the Methodists' presiding bishop, plus scores of priests, ministers and rabbis. Swarming around us were hundreds of reporters and cameramen from all over the world. Further, behind the scenes there had been intense negotiating going on all night to prevent another confrontation.

The deal, it turned out, was that Dr. King would lead us across the bridge, allow us to be stopped, and then turn around. This would cover three bases at once: it would satisfy our need to stand up to police terror; it gave the troopers the chance to – peaceably – reassert their version of law and order; and Dr. King had reason to believe the excursion would not be counted as defiance of the court order. But of course, anything could happen, so we were all appropriately somber as we stepped off.

Publicly, Governor Wallace remained belligerent; but when I interviewed him years later, he said that after the Sunday attack, he had already called in trooper commander Al Lingo and fired him for defying orders on Bloody Sunday. The announcement of Lingo's departure was put off for several months, however, so it would not be obviously connected with the march.

Except for one hitch, the scenario went off as planned. The troopers let Dr. King and the notables pass over and just beyond the bridge, then stopped them on cue. Behind them, our ranks stretched all the way back across it into downtown. Dr. King affirmed our right to march, and the trooper in charge told him we couldn't, that we must return to the church; again, all as planned. We knelt and prayed, then rose to go.

At that moment, the troopers were abruptly ordered to move back and off the road. All at once, Highway 80 lay open before us, stretching east toward Montgomery without obstruction.

This sudden withdrawal was not on the program, and I still wonder why it happened. Was Wallace trying to tempt King into defiance of the court order by going beyond the agreed upon boundary? Was the governor once more being double-crossed by his own men? Or were he and they waiting for King to move ahead so they could attack again?

We'll never know, because Dr. King did not rise to the bait. He turned around and we marched back to Brown Chapel. Some murmured angrily at what seemed like a needless retreat, but most of us were relieved to be getting back to the church in one piece.

VII

Whatever the ambiguities of that second march across the bridge, it didn't take long for the situation to heat up again: James Reeb, a Unitarian minister from Boston who had flown in to join the march, was attacked by white hoodlums near a downtown cafe, and left with a skull fracture and blood clot that would kill him within two days.

While Reeb lingered, the outcry against his beating was international, dwarfing by far the mostly local reaction to Jimmie Lee Jackson's death; but that's white culture for you, and in any case, the anger was quickly turned to the movement's benefit.

Wednesday a march poured out of Brown Chapel, along with a battalion of reporters, headed to the courthouse for a protest vigil in Reeb's honor. They were stopped halfway down the block by a solid phalanx of troopers and sheriff's possemen.

The marchers, among them many notables who had made the bridge crossing the day before, were ready. For the next several hours, one after another stepped forward to harangue the troopers and preach to the world. And after a break for dinner, marchers returned to the street, where troopers and possemen still stood, now behind a rope strung across Sylvan Street by Wilson Baker. The rope, instantly dubbed the Berlin Wall, became the focus of a nonstop vigil that lasted almost six days.

This week of the vigil was among the most intense and exalted of the Selma campaign. Hundreds of ministers, priests, nuns, bishops, rabbis and other church people came streaming in and through Selma, filling the church for what seemed like endless mass meetings. Again and again these pilgrims were astonished and moved, just as I had been that night in Atlanta during the Scripto strike – was it really only three months earlier?– by the spirit of the movement, the power of its singing, the eloquence of its oratory, all of which were then at a kind of peak. There is even reason to believe that traces of its impact seeped under the barricades and affected some of the troopers. In any event, they were soon being spelled by conservation officers and liquor control cops.

It was a good week for me too, because I stumbled into a useful substitute for my failed journalistic mission: I became a chauffeur. To deal with the steady stream of newcomers flying in to Montgomery, SCLC rented several cars, and I managed to commandeer one. I happily spent most of those days ferrying various notables, most of whom I had never heard of, back and forth to the airport.

The car brought more than a hint of luxury to my $25 per week standard of living: it was warm, new, and had a good radio. It also served as a useful stage: for a series of rapt, terrified passengers, I turned the journey down Highway 80 into an instant history tour. If I was unable to write, I could still talk, and talk I did, starting with the full-size John Birch Society billboard near the airport, which demanded that we "Get the US OUT of the UN," and do it now. Then:

"Yes, this is Lowndes County, where no blacks are registered; they say the last black man who tried to register there was shot dead on the courthouse steps; that's what they say.

"And there–see that ramshackle old building? It's a real, functioning one-room schoolhouse (well, three rooms actually), with holes in the floor and walls that let in the winter wind; that's right, it's all the public education available for Negroes in the county."

Twenty or so white-knuckled miles later:

"And don't miss that bank billboard there, the one that welcomes us to Selma as 'the city with 100 per cent human interest.' Look to the other side, and there's another for the White Citizens Council (a pause for gasps); and they're both located just about at the spot where the troopers attacked the march–they hid their horses behind that building over there."

By then, eyes were wide, necks craned.

Once across the bridge, we turned right at the courthouse,

where I casually mentioned my arrests and the close encounter with the possemen's cattle prods, cruised cautiously past City Hall, describing the two jails it housed, and then jogged again to get to Sylvan Street and the church.

Once the rope was up and the vigil was on, we couldn't go directly there; I had to circle around to Jeff Davis and come up from the other direction, and to drop off my passengers, who by now were usually half-dazed with awe at the apocalyptic spectacle they were joining.

One trip turned out differently, though. At the Montgomery airport, looking for the Selma contingent, I saw a stunning blonde, dressed in demure but elegant black, coming toward me. She flashed a winsome smile, said something about coming from Michigan, and asked for a ride to the church.

With *pleasure,* ma'am, I thought, and welcome to the Southland.

She insisted on sitting up front with me, and listened to my tourist spiel with a semblance of interest. I had some trouble getting through it, though, because she was so good to look at; the black suit, despite its modest cut, only set off her full figure. Then as we approached the bridge, she interrupted to ask if I knew where Dr. King was.

I shrugged. Maybe at the church, maybe somewhere else, I wasn't sure.

But she persisted. She wanted to see Dr. King. She needed to see him. That, she said, was why she came.

Well, let me think; it was midday, the mass meetings were probably in a lull, and Dr. King could be conferring with staff in the back of the church, or possibly resting somewhere – I knew of an apartment in the projects nearby where he often slipped away for some quiet. But he might be somewhere else entirely, coming back later–

But where is he *now?* She insisted. I need to see him.

All at once my guard was up. Who was this woman? What was she after? She did not seem acquainted with Dr. King or the movement. But the very elegance of her appearance, I realized, exuded an unspoken awareness of Dr. King's fondness for female pulchritude. And her sense of mission reinforced my sudden suspicion. She seemed to presume he would want to talk with her, be with her; and she might well have been right.

But for what purpose? The steady stream of death threats came rushing back to me. Most were no more than racist invective; but I knew some, like the one aimed at the aborted night march in February, had been real. And for a serious, skillful assassination plan, there would be more than one way to get close to him, to bait a fatal trap.

My responses to her queries became suddenly vague; my tour guide banter subsided into bumpkin monosyllables. I managed to get quite close to the church, pulled up, and pointed toward the back of the church. "The offices are there." I doubted Dr. King was inside; but if he was, he'd surely be surrounded by staff, with dozens of reporters and photographers close by.

She thanked me, snatched up her small travel bag, and was gone, pushing her way into the crowd milling around outside the building.

That was that; I never saw or heard of her again, and whatever happened, Dr. King survived.

VIII

As the days passed, though, tension again began to rise. After lengthy hearings, federal judge Frank Johnson ordered that the march be permitted, under state protection. Governor Wallace immediately began maneuvering to hand off the job of protecting the march to Washington, while maintaining an outward stance of defiance of federal invaders.

But he was up against one of the canniest of antagonists in Lyndon Johnson, and the President won the public relations battle: Wallace sent him a letter complaining that protecting the march would be too expensive for the state. Johnson responded by calling in reporters, reading the letter to them, pointing out that Wallace had the Alabama National Guard at his disposal for just such duties. Then Johnson added that if the governor would not call up the Guard, he would.

In Selma, tensions between Wilson Baker and Sheriff Clark ratcheted steadily toward the breaking point. One night, I learned later, the two had come to blows, and Mayor Smitherman had to pull them apart. We didn't know this in Brown Chapel, but the tension in the air was palpable. One evening, returning from Montgomery with a load of passengers, I found this out when we were stopped by state troopers a block away from the church. Afterward, I put the encounter down in verse form:

The trooper car is, of course, waiting when you get back to your
    car:
"Hey you" (flashlight beam, reflections off uniform brass, neck
    hairs fluorescent in headlight glare) "where you think you're
    goin?"
To freedom. To heaven (to hell?) To anywhere. To–
"To the church." (clear your throat quickly so your voice doesn't
    falter) Yes, of course: to the church.
"Lessee your identification and the registration on that car. . . ."
Pull out the wallet and start the charade, let them examine your
    driver's license etc., with extreme and exaggerated care, of
    course they have to get on the radio and check the car out
    through Birmingham, outside agitators are an unsavory lot
    and it's more than likely stolen;
But while you're standing there, looking carefully off down the
    nighttime street, notice the other trooper looking at you
intently, *intently:*
"Where you from, Charles?" (listen to the question: something
    rings in it besides antagonism, there is more than one query
    in the words; look up at him quick, how can you answer
    without exposing the concealed questions?)
"Well (you want to say give me thirty seconds to think over my
    answer(s) at least)–"
"What," interrupts the other trooper, "does that button mean?"
    and he points:

GROW–white letters on black background, Get Rid Of Wallace, what else, but you won't say that, you don't need to get beat up tonight, and besides you know that he asked it because he too heard some (not all) of the other questions in his partner's voice; so you have to answer him satisfactorily without letting it tear down the little bridge the other has extended.
"Well. . . GROW refers to the philosophy of the whole movement . . . " etc., etc., and so on, it's hard, but the other trooper is still peering so the bridge is still there.
"MmmminmHhmmmm," the questioner says; he of course knows what it really means, but your straightfaced baloney throws him temporarily off balance. Silence in heaven (and earth) for the space of about half an hour (minute). Then–
"Where'd you say you were from?" Listen again:
Reach out:
"Well, I was born" (yes I hear you) "and then we went" (can you give me your hand?) "and after that we" (just for a moment) "when I finished college–"
He nods a little and you know he heard; so did the other, and his guard is up:
– "Why don't you get a good job back where you came from, and quit messin' around down here?"
It was too good to last. . . . Just try to retreat with dignity and without burning the bridge's remains. . . .
"Yeah, there''s other ways to settle this than in the street," the other, his guard also now up, joins in. . .
There isn't any answer for this, so just look down at the muddy street.
He hands you back your license and finishes up the charade:
"Tell your boss to get some identification on this car, and we're

not letting anybody into the church. Only the sheriff could do that."

IX

Under Judge Johnson's order, a maximum of 300 persons would be permitted to make the full five-day, fifty-mile march from Selma to Montgomery. This limit made sense for the work of protecting the group while they were on the two-lane, often swampy and overgrown stretch of Highway 80 through Lowndes County. For the first leg, however, over the Pettus bridge and east to the county line, the limit was lifted, as it would also be for the final stretch, where the road divided to four lanes as it approached the capital city.

The trek began again on March twenty-first, and this time it was for real. It had taken several days of frantic, makeshift preparations to make it possible. A big crowd crossed the bridge with the select 300, and I happily joined in

Pacifists that many of us ostensibly were, few of us in the ranks were sorry to see the well-armed and vigilant U.S. Army troops lining the highway, or the olive drab helicopters churning overhead. Again, a passel of notables was at the front of the group, but the one I recall most vividly was a tall, lithe woman dressed to the nines as if strolling up Fifth Avenue, sticking out like an elegantly turned out sore thumb.

This was Renata Adler of the *New Yorker*, notebook in hand preparing an appropriately titled "Letter from Selma," for that magazine. She fell in beside me for a few paces, long enough to get my name for her piece, while I was waving at some of the angry whites shouting at us from the sidelines, inviting them to get over it and march with us.

I was not, of course, part of the 300, but tagged along nonetheless to the first night's campsite, on a friendly farmer's land. There we found tents and grub, the food consisting of shiny new trash cans full of pork and beans and spaghetti. We also found frost; it was cold, and a series of big kerosene heaters had been brought in, and their blowers were turned on, to take the edge off the chill.

Smelling the fumes from these heaters, I became alarmed. What about carbon monoxide? Weren't we putting the marchers at risk, expecting them to lie down with that stuff blowing on them all night? As the smell from the heaters' exhaust became more oppressive, I got ever more worried: something terrible was about to happen. I asked around – were these contraptions safe? No one seemed to know. Everyone's focus seemed to be on food and sore feet.

Finally I couldn't take it anymore: a disaster was imminent, and somebody had to stop it. I went around one tent, flipping off the switches on the heaters, and shouting for someone to raise the tent flaps and allow some real air in, before people started asphyxiating.

Naturally, with the fresh air came the cold, and protests from other marchers. Someone finally found James Bevel, who assumed command of the situation. He listened to my fears, then called for advice from one of the crew that had set up the camp. The crew member shook his head and assured him that the heaters smelled bad, but weren't going to hurt anybody; the tents, after all, were hardly airtight.

Bevel was diplomatic, thanking me for my concern for the marchers' safety, but directing that the heaters be fired up again. I slunk away, embarrassed at my over-reaction, and relieved in any case to be headed back to a real bed for the night. And of course, the crew was right: the heaters didn't suffocate anyone.

I managed to slip back one other time and march through part of the swampy stretch in Lowndes County, but mostly I spent those days doing my taxi bit, passing the marchers at a crawl each way, under the watchful eyes of the troops. The last night of the march a big crowd gathered near Montgomery to hear a succession of big-name entertainers at a hastily organized concert. The next morning, Tish and I joined the thousands who surrounded the 300 and converged on the alabaster capitol to hear Dr. King reach for one of his rhythmic perorations: "How Long? Not long?"

Chapter Six
Vietnam Rising

I

The story of the march and its climax has been told in more detail elsewhere, not least in my own book, *Selma 1965*, and I don't want to repeat myself here any more than necessary. It was frightening, but not really unexpected, to wake up the next morning and hear that a woman marcher from Detroit, Mrs. Viola Liuzzo, had been gunned down on Highway 80 in Lowndes County, by a group of Klansmen.

Despite the blast of publicity surrounding this latest killing, the local aftermath of the march to Montgomery was a long, messy ebbing of energy and focus. That was true for Tish and me, as it was for the community and the movement.

The actual scene of action rapidly shifted to Washington, where Congress moved with what was for that body amazing speed toward passage of the Voting Rights Act. In Selma, the dignitaries and visiting preachers packed up and headed home, while the reporters moved on to the next exciting location.

Within SCLC, attention turned to the sequel to Selma, and the question sparked weeks of infighting. On the one side was Hosea, who argued that SCOPE should be the main focus through the summer. In line with that, he asked for authority over all the field staff, including those in Alabama, which meant us. On the other side, Bevel insisted that the march to Montgomery had been just a curtain-raiser to much more militant protests, which would culminate in mass arrests and a demand for new, "free elections" in the state.

Bevel's strategic insight, which had seemed so sure a few weeks before, failed him utterly now. The black people of Selma and Alabama had just seen something that was the functional equivalent of the parting of the Red Sea. Their energies were spent, and they were still taking in the magnitude of what had happened. It was completely at variance with this sense to tell them that all they had seen so far was merely the prelude to even bigger, more militant actions. Bevel, to speak frankly, had no clue.

There was yet a third strain emerging in this internal debate: the idea that SCLC should move north for its next major campaign. Dr. King and Andy Young were increasingly interested in mounting a campaign in either New York or Chicago, with Chicago the early favorite. Still, a Northern foray would take time to prepare, so that possibility remained in the talking stage at this point.

For us in Selma, the uncertainty at the upper levels of SCLC left us adrift. At the same time, an unsolicited stream of money and materiel had begun flowing into the city. Soon the large basement of First Baptist Church, a block down from Brown Chapel, was jammed with piles of canned goods and other stuff. I personally fielded calls from a rabbi in Maine who promised he could send us thousands of pairs of new shoes, if only I could guarantee that Dr. King would speak at a rally in his home town to accept them. He called his project Operation Heart-to-Heart. (I wondered if it wouldn't more rightly be dubbed Operation Soul-to-Sole. But in any case, I couldn't guarantee anything about Dr. King, and the shoes did not materialize.)

Although the supplies were sent as an expression of compassion, and there was in fact widespread need in the area, the black community was not equipped to handle this influx. While some hungry people may have been fed, the effects on the community at large, at least as far as I could see, were mostly destructive: turf battles, allegations of theft and profiteering, power struggles and eventually, arrests.

What I saw there for the first time has been confirmed many times since: it is by no means an easy or risk-free undertaking for wealthy people to "help" those in need at a distance. Compassion that is not closely aligned with skill and discernment begets mainly waste, strife, and often worse.

Which is not to say that Tish and I were above reaping our own small benefits from this outpouring. We were soon invited

North by people we had met during the crowded days of the march, and made something of a triumphal tour that spring, visiting New York (where I was refused entrance to the United Nations building because my movement overalls, which were deemed inappropriate by the security guard), then being feted at Yale (put up in VIP guest rooms in one of their ornate residential colleges), and finally moving up to Boston where we saw one of my walking buddies from Camp Selma, Gordon Gibson.

II

Of course, it was fun being a minor celebrity, spinning yarns to rapt groups of students and churchpeople about facing the deputies with their cattle prods, and spending time in jail. But in Boston, there was a key moment of another sort: Gordon Gibson took me to Boston University, where a large meeting of clergy had gathered to hear a debate about the Vietnam War.

I went into the meeting with somewhat of an open mind:. My Marxist readings in Camp Selma had softened my inherited military and anti-communist reflexes up a bit, but they were hardly gone. And despite paying close attention to Dr. King's words and example, I was innocent of the implications, if any, of his nonviolence for international conflicts.

A panel of three was assembled to speak to us. One was a Cornell professor, George McT. Kahin, an area specialist; the second was from the State Department, a rumpled, semi-ambassadorial-looking fellow who smoked nonstop and whose name escaped me; the third was Philip Berrigan, then still a priest of the Josephite order, which worked mainly in black communities.

I can't recall who went first, but each one made a distinct, even indelible impression: Berrigan, dressed in priestly black, was a predictable firebrand, calling on us to denounce and act against the war at the peril of our consciences – nay, our immortal souls.

The Cornell professor was– well, professorial, but keenly informed and full of facts which added up to a calmly damning portrait of the historical and policy follies that had led us into the morass of war.

But it was the State Department representative who tipped the balance for me. He took the podium, flashed a smile marred by tobacco stains visible even as far back as we were sitting, then started out by patronizing us as the keepers and embodiments of the Judeo-Christian heritage. Then he launched into a spiel defending the war which, sentence by sentence, became not only less convincing but even counterproductive.

I don't remember his specifics: doubtless he talked about the Domino theory, the threat of Chinese communism, and the necessity of supporting the President and our troops. But beyond the verbal message there was the presentation, which reeked of corruption and decadence, combined with arrogance and condescension, that I could see was making many in the audience angrier every minute it continued. Our job, we were in effect being told, was to pray and tend the fires of the Judeo-Christian heritage; meantime, he and his sort, the real men, would continue to run the world.

Maybe if the State Department had chosen its spokesmen better, many things would have been different for me; but I doubt it. He was, after all, speaking in Boston, to the heirs of the abolitionist preachers who had made slavery a fighting issue. Telling such a group that their sort were to have no real role in this grave national matter of life and death was probably doomed from the start.

He was also confirming, right before my eyes, the thesis of Colonel Bexield's honors seminar at CSU two years before: that a big country will intervene militarily in a smaller one when it damn well pleases, and when it thinks it can get away with it.

If I entered that auditorium with some semblance of an open mind about the war, when we left, scarcely two hours later, I was dead-set against it. Communism worried me less than what I had seen and heard from the representative of my own government. What this sudden realization would lead to was by no means certain. But one thing was, namely that the U.S. government would have to reckon with me and others like me over Vietnam, one way or another, and soon.

II

Back in Selma, southern summer weather had arrived: enervating heat and humidity, dust hanging over the unpaved streets of the black neighborhoods, with the only consolations being occasional thunderstorms and long, lovely dusks as the light slanted through the trees on its leisurely way to nightfall.

And with the approach of summer there came also the question of what to do about SCOPE. Hosea Williams' big grant application, had been approved, and Bevel's plans for another round of mass demonstrations had evaporated. But where this left us was still unclear. One day a sleek rental car SCOPE had paid for pulled up outside our house on Lapsley Street. The driver, one of Hosea's assistants named Stoney Cooks, emerged from it to tell Tish and me that Hosea wanted us on his team. Stoney also acknowledged that we were not obliged to join with it.

There were big plans for SCOPE, we were assured: organizers would be fanning out across the South, leading platoons of volunteers in a blitz of community organizing and political education which would easily outshine the already-legendary Mississippi Freedom Summer of the year before.

Tish and I were skeptical. We did not doubt Hosea's dedication and courage; he had after all led the first march across the bridge, into the teeth of the troopers and possemen, after losing the coin toss with Andy Young. But the truth was, neither of us liked him much personally. He was hard to work with, as I had found in Atlanta when we tangled over the draft of the SCOPE proposal. And what about his organizational abilities? Would he actually be able to pull off his ambitious, region-wide program? Who was going to train all these volunteers? Who would ride herd on them once they were in the field?

What we knew of the staff Hosea had assembled for these tasks was not impressive: they were few in number, not the most highly regarded or experienced, and seemed very devoted to the personal spending on air travel, cars, motels and restaurants made possible by this huge chunk of someone else's money. We told Stoney we would think it over; but we were not seriously tempted, and when he came back, our answer was a quiet but firm No.

Our apprehensions were soon confirmed. SCOPE's money was quickly spent, in much the same ways we expected; tales of bacchanals and big-ticket goofing off were soon circulating through the movement grapevine; and the actual work done in the counties by volunteers was sparse, spotty, and little noted. The

Mississippi Summer Project remained by far the more impressive achievement.

But saying No to SCOPE left open the question of what we were to do. Tish worked fitfully in the movement office downtown, doing secretarial chores and fending off the advances of the male staffers. My role was even more vague; Selma was out of the mainstream now, so there was hardly any news for me to write up for Atlanta, even if I had overcome my "reporter's block" and been able to do it, which I hadn't. While pro forma efforts to get local blacks registered continued, there was little real energy behind them. We were really in a holding pattern, waiting for Congress to pass a Voting Rights Act which would, we fully expected, sweep away the old system and its clumsy machinery entirely.

But while we sweated in the Alabama heat, Congress seemed to be taking its time. We had expected to see the law enacted by June; in fact, it was not signed until August. Again, for such a major piece of legislation to clear both houses and reach President Johnson's desk in a mere six months was a remarkable feat, truly amazing speed for the "world's greatest deliberative bodies." But the summer hiatus meant long days and weeks of inertia and drift for those "in the field."

It was also, in fairness to Hosea, a major blow to his hopes for SCOPE. He expected his volunteers would be lining up people to register by the tens of thousands under the new law; but by the time it was enacted, most of the volunteers were preparing to head home, or had already left.

III

In Selma, our situation was briefly enlivened after the phone rang one day and a voice said to me, "Chuck, it's Jim! From San Francisco. Remember?"

In truth, I didn't. During the frenzied days leading up to the March to Montgomery, I had met dozens of people, from all corners of the nation, both traveling back and forth in my airport chauffeur's role, and in numerous intense conversations in and around Brown Chapel. Except for a few, particularly those I had been in jail with, many of the faces and names ran together in my memory.

Jim wasn't offended by having to remind me. He was an activist graduate student at San Francisco State College, who had raised lots of money for SNCC and the Mississippi Freedom Summer. He had told me about all this when he came to Selma to join the march. Like many others, he had asked me what he could do when he got back home, to show support and keep the momentum going.

I had told him, he said, that he should collect and send books; and I had also spoken about wanting to see a Freedom School in Selma that summer. In Mississippi there had reportedly been many such Freedom Schools, staffed by northern volunteers who taught classes in various basic, liberating subjects to rooms full of quiet, receptive men and women of color.

I recalled all this only vaguely; there had been so many people, and so many conversations. . . .

But Jim informed me he had taken my counsel to heart, returned home from Montgomery to a hero's welcome, and with an experienced organizer's skill had leveraged this attention into concrete action. He had, he said, collected a truckload of books, several hundred dollars, and had signed up half a dozen volunteers, all of whom were primed to come to Selma as soon as I gave the word, to set up and run a Freedom School open to all ages. He even had a name for it, which had been very useful in his work on campus: Selma Free College. All I had to do was tell him where to direct the truck, and find a place where we could hold the classes.

Well. This was pretty breathtaking news. It also, with a stroke, reshaped and revived my own situation: I was no longer adrift. Now I had a mission: to be the godfather and overseer of a genuine Freedom School. Even though Jim had done all the work, within the movement I could claim the credit; it would be my baby.

To make good on this coup, though, I did need to find a home for the project. And this did not prove to be an easy task. Brown Chapel, for instance, had secured a place in history as the headquarters of the movement at its peak; but both its building and its congregation had suffered considerable wear and tear in its months of involvement, and there was no great willingness there to open up again for the summer. Down the street, First Baptist Church was still grappling with a basement full of canned goods, and the squabbles they had produced. At other churches, there were other sorts of reluctance. I was getting nowhere fast.

Finally, with time growing short, I heard about an unused church building a few blocks from Brown Chapel, on a shabby block of Green Street, and hurried to check it out. It looked ideal: open space inside, shelves for storing supplies, some chairs and benches which we could move around. From the outside it was dilapidated-looking, the paint long since worn off its clapboard exterior. But we could fix it up; and the price was modest, something like $50 for the summer. I gladly paid the ancient elder who unlocked it for me, and he handed over the key.

One of Jim's volunteers had family in Yellow Springs, Ohio, which is almost due north of Selma, only a few states but several light years away, and in early summer we drove up there to meet the crew and get organized.

Our prospects looked excellent: the volunteers were an interesting and varied crew, all anxious to get started; one of them turned out to have a wealthy father, also from Ohio, who took a personal interest in our project and seemed ready to serve as an angel, providing us with timely infusions of cash as the need arose. We headed back to Selma, ready for a summer of productive adventure.

IV

Our time on Green Street turned out to be brief, however. No sooner had we attempted to move in than we were assailed by a gaggle of pre-teen boys, known informally as the Green Street Gang.

This was not a "gang" in the more recent, more organized and violent sense of the term, but rather like something out of the Little Rascals, but with edge and attitude. Like so many others, these kids were on the loose with little to do. They wanted attention, they wanted the goodies we were bringing, and in their small, rundown turf they did not want to take no for an answer.

"Come on, Chuck, don't be so hard," they taunted when I declined to give them money or more cookies. I insisted that the supplies were for our classes, and would be distributed in an orderly way, on our schedule.

Our image was of a lively but polite playgroup during the morning, complete with snacks, coloring books and probably some singing. Tish was interested in that; I was looking forward to adult classes in the evening.

But we never really got a chance to act out our liberal daydream. The day after we first moved into the church, we returned to find the door had been jimmied and our cookie stash raided. The Green Street boys swarmed around, snickering brazenly over their easy breach of our fortress and wanting more of what we had.

I resisted. We needed to establish a modicum of order. How could we have any program if we couldn't at least secure the building? Who was in charge here, after all? We had paid rent.

I got a new, bigger padlock for the front door; but that night they came in through one of the windows. Then I nailed up wire screening over the lower windows; the next day we saw they had ripped loose a corner and got in again.

The downward spiral was quick and evident. The climax of sorts came a few days later, after Tish came upon a hungry kitten wandering past, scruffy, mewling and abandoned. We already had a black tomcat at home, whom we jokingly referred to as a "baby surrogate," and Tish's reaction to the orphaned kitten was immediate and maternal. She brought it into the church, went for some milk, and cleaned its fur, fussing and cooing over it.

When asked about its provenance, the hovering Green Street boys were unsentimental: "I'on' know," they shrugged. "Who cares? It's just a cat."

We couldn't take the kitten home; Mrs. Boynton would not approve, and anyway I knew that tomcats like ours regarded kittens as no more than animated snacks. So Tish locked our new pet in the church, complete with a cardboard carton made up as a bed, a makeshift catbox and more milk to lap at.

The following morning the window screen had been pulled loose again, as usual. Inside, the cat hostel had been kicked over, and its occupant had disappeared. An anxious search around the building soon ensued, and before long we found it. The kitten had been stomped to death, blood from its small mouth congealing in the dust.

As Tish cried and I stood by helplessly, the Green Street gang circled around, demanding and taunting: "C'mon, Chuck, gimme a dollar, hey don't be so hard, Chuck it's only a cat, hey gimme fifty cents, c'mon Chuck, why you gotta be so *hard*?"

V

That was the effective end of our tenure on Green Street. Tish and I soon quarreled about the program, and she retreated to the office downtown, refusing to have anything further to do with the school project.

But I didn't know what to do either. I had gone home after the kitten's demise and wrote a poem about it, which has unfortunately been lost. I was acutely aware of the ambiguity of our position there, the white do-gooders out of our depth, up against feral street kids who wondered rightly, if destructively, why we were so much more solicitous and indulgent of a stray animal than we were of them. Within a few days, we abandoned the church to the Green Street gang, who I am sure promptly lost interest in it as well.

With the loss of our base, the hope of a coherent program for the Selma Free College vanished too. There were a few positive signs of its existence, however: a couple of adult classes did get started in another church, as some of the other volunteers showed considerably more organizing savvy than did I.

We managed even better with the truckload of books Jim had delivered. A local black service club offered us the use of an unoccupied house near the black high school for a Freedom Library, and even installed shelving for the collection. For more than a year afterward, the house was opened once or twice a week by a local volunteer, and often swarmed with teenagers coming and going from school. If they were better at borrowing the books than returning them, that was all right with us.

But program or no program, what would our freedom school project be without its own staff soap operas? It wasn't long before some developed.

There was, for instance, Jay, a tall fellow who hailed from Minnesota, and hadn't been in San Francisco all that long. Jay was drop-dead handsome, with a model's good looks. I was later told that Jay actually had been a model, for one of those kitschy church calendars featuring the long-haired Nordic Christ, and I could believe it – he absolutely had the look.

Jay also seemed rather a sophisticate, able to home in on what was what and who was who around town. But I didn't find this out until our Ohio benefactor flew in for a visit. We were hoping for a windfall from him, and gathered to discuss how best to show him the town and put the best face on our somewhat scattered efforts. Jay said he knew just where to take him for dinner, a special quiet place he had found, called Marie's, I think.

I had never heard of Marie's, and was curious to know more. And as local "coordinator," I was naturally to come along.

When the benefactor arrived in Montgomery, we drove him back to town while I gave him my travelogue spiel, and he was suitably impressed. Then Jay took over and guided us to what turned out to be a sizeable but unassuming house in the heart of one of the black sections of town.

There was no sign identifying it as a restaurant, but we were greeted warmly at the door by a woman I took to be Marie. She led us into a large, candlelit dining room in which there were several small tables, tastefully covered with white tablecloths, and took our orders herself.

The food was good, with a distinctly home-cooked presentation. As we chatted and ate, I noticed other couples coming into the room, sitting quietly together in the dim, flickering light, drinking and talking, and then leaving one by one. Our party seemed to be the only sizeable one, and the only group focused primarily on a meal.

By the time we finished, the light was beginning to dawn, and when we had dropped off our guest, Jay smilingly confirmed my suspicion: Marie's was indeed a brothel, and the lady who had greeted us was the madame.

But so what? Jay said. It was a quiet, dignified establishment, and the food – we all agreed – had been excellent. Besides, Jay chuckled, our Ohio visitor never suspected a thing. We all laughed with him.

Except that the visitor had. As a successful businessman, he had his own sophistication; and Ohio is not such a backward place either. A few days after he left, a letter came announcing that he was bailing out of backing our project. He wrote carefully and elliptically, praising our idealistic dedication, but the underlying implication was plain enough: in a strange town, where outsiders were subject to arrest and harassment, we had taken him, a man with a reputation to worry about, to a whorehouse.

What if Jim Clark had chosen that night to raid the place? None of us had partaken of anything more sensual than Marie's sweet potato pie; but had our friend's name come over the newswire, would a reporter for the Akron *Beacon-Journal* or the Cleveland *Plain Dealer* have cared about that?

We still giggled over the whole thing, including my naivete; but that was the end of his patronage, and not long thereafter, his daughter pulled out and headed home as well.

Our ranks thus reduced, we carried on as best we could. But another tangle soon surfaced. One of the other volunteers, I'll call her Gloria, had a strong attachment to Jay. Gloria was tall and gangly, with frizzy hair and a voice that was loud and usually urgent in tone. It seemed that everywhere Jay went, Gloria was sure to go, and while I didn't see signs of actual passion, I began to infer that they must be something of a couple.

But then in midsummer, from out of nowhere a newcomer appeared on our scene: Anne, a nurse from Milwaukee.

Anne was quiet and lovely, willowy and graceful, with dark hair usually pulled back in a roll that was conservative but appealing. She had an air of soft-spoken confidence that bespoke an assured professional, yet was not overbearing. She had not, she explained, come to join our Selma Free College, much as she admired our stumbling efforts. Instead, she admitted candidly, she had come for Jay.

It turned out Anne was Jay's fiancee; or at least she had been, until he abruptly decamped westward. The soap opera details of this saga were never entirely clear to me, but seemed to come down to Jay's having fled in panic from the prospect of settling down to bourgeois wedlock and Wisconsin respectability. It was a variation on a story many an immigrant to San Francisco could tell.

But Anne, while spurned, was not to be denied. She had somehow traced Jay's movements, and once he had left the protective underbrush of Golden Gate culture for Selma's relatively confined precincts, she made her move. Anne was the picture of magnanimity: prepared to understand and forgive Jay's shrinking at the altar of adulthood, ready to take him back, and to take him back home.

Most of us were charmed and fascinated by this unfolding tale; and Jay, the seeming sophisticate, confirmed it wordlessly by suddenly appearing hangdog and embarrassed in Anne's presence, like a boy caught playing hooky.

The main dissenter, of course, was Gloria, who saw her hopes of snaring Jay quickly going up in smoke. She was loud, she was angry, she was vehement. Anne was an interloper at best, she insisted, and an impostor at worst; Jay was now free to make his own choices, free to choose to be with her.

But Anne, for all her soft-spoken, even genteel calm, was steely in her resolve, and it was soon clear that neither Gloria, nor Jay for that matter, was a match for her. In a few days they were headed north, Anne radiant and serene and Jay sheepish when we last saw them. I wonder occasionally what ever became of them. Gloria left shortly afterward, headed west with her grief.

VI

Once the dust from this melodrama had settled, there wasn't much left of our bravely titled Selma Free College. We had no home, having been run out of Green Street; only a couple volunteers were left, teaching occasional classes in a church here and there, and otherwise at loose ends. The library was our main achievement, but it was also the least demanding of anyone's time because of the local support. The hot days wore on, and in Washington the Voting Rights Act inched toward Lyndon Johnson's desk, but hadn't arrived there yet.

All of which allowed my own uncertainties and confusion to surface again. Tish and I quarreled frequently in those days, and ended up seeking counseling help. To find it we began driving to a clinic in Birmingham; it was two hours away, but we had to go that far to feel safe.

The therapist we saw there was not exactly a warm fuzzy

comforter; we were still several years away from the human potential preoccupations of the Seventies. Once when I asked him for a diagnosis of my situation, he turned to an assistant and snapped, "Adjustment Reaction to Adulthood." I suspect it was an accurate enough verdict, but it sounded sarcastic and almost trivial; didn't I even have a real neurosis to struggle with?

To his credit, he quickly picked up on this self-pity. In one session, I was complaining that our existence in Selma in these dog days didn't seem significant, nor did the immediate prospects.

He interrupted my monologue to ask sharply, "Tell me —do you feel *in*significant?"

The truth was, I did. I was a fake and a failure in my original assignment for SCLC, having written nothing of consequence for them; further, the collapse of the Selma Free College project, and the doldrums which beset the voter organizing, were equally dispiriting.

For that matter, even the certainty of eventual passage of the Voting Rights Act, while it was bound to revive the registration effort, didn't bring me any personal cheer. That was because, if my time in Alabama had taught me nothing else, it had shown me I was not really cut out to be a community organizer. I had pitched in, of course, followed along with my movement mentors; and when I had managed to help "turn out" the students from Selma University, had actually scored something of a bloop hit in the organizer's game.

But these experiences, illuminated by the aftermath of the March to Montgomery, had made it clear that organizing as an ongoing effort demanded a temperament that I just did not possess. I wanted to read, to think, to talk and write; outward experience, even the intense days of the campaign, were grist for my inward mill, for reflection and analysis.

In this form there resurfaced the fork in the road I had confronted the previous autumn while juggling the job at the Atlanta *Journal* and my interest in SCLC: whether to be part of the movement, or to report on, understand, and analyze it? After the fateful Scripto mass meeting, the choice had seemed clear. But maybe that had only been true for a time; maybe now I was reverting to type, a more basic type.

In time this introvert's temperament would be confirmed and

named by the machinery of the Meyers-Briggs test and other psychological paraphernalia; but now all I knew was that an organizer is in large measure a salesman, who talks a lot, but keeps on the move, knocking on a lot of doors, working intensively with people to help them overcome their fears and join with others to protest and change their circumstances – and that wasn't me.

It wasn't that I disdained or condescended to such work; hardly. The better I understood it, the more I admired the organizer's craft. But at the same time, I could look around Selma, where the veteran SCLC and SNCC staff still labored, and then see beyond it to the wide dusty fields and winding back roads of the surrounding Black belt counties, and be increasingly sure that I was not meant to spend my productive years there, following their example.

And this is not to mention the fact, of which I was now fully aware, that it was hardly a white person's place to be doing the black community's organizing. Whites could help, sometimes, in subordinate roles. SCLC had always included a few whites on its staff. SNCC had too, but by 1965 its ethos was changing fast. The sentiment that was to break the surface in another year in the slogan "Black power" was already widespread internally, and I knew what it meant. If I wanted to stay in the South and be an organizer, I would have to learn how to work primarily with whites.

But personality aside, that prospect was equally discouraging, because I was not a white Southerner, and the depth of that cultural gap was becoming clear to me. How long would it take me to assimilate to the white world around me, and what would be the psychic costs? By now I could mimic a southern accent well enough to "pass" as local when a state trooper stopped us on one of our trips to Birmingham; and I was acquiring a taste for some regional foods – grits and RC Cola come to mind – but these were mere beginnings.

White southern religiosity was another kettle of fish entirely. I loved the singing and the energy of the black churches; but when a white gospel quartet intruded onto the local airwaves, the nasal whines and sentimentality made me cringe.

Was this simple prejudice? To this day, I don't know. On the one hand, I tell myself that southern black religion, with its context of slavery, reaches great depths despite all the preacherly chicanery and showmanship; the spirituals, for instance, seem about as close to authentic scripture that indigenous American spiritual literature has produced.

— But then, I retort, what about the long suffering of generations of poor southern whites? Is their history of privation any less "authentic"?

How can I say it isn't? They are just as human, as beloved by God, if there is one, and suffering is suffering, is it not? The logic, the morality here seems unanswerable.

And so I stump myself, at least rationally; but my feelings were and are still clear, and not at all even-handed or dispassionate: no white gospel quartet ever moved me half as much as any one of a dozen unknown black soloists on the platform at Brown Chapel, who gave voice to the pain, faith and courage that made the movement move.

Besides which, while I left Catholicism behind in high school, Rome had marked me deeply enough that the whole Protestant enterprise, and in particular its white southern incarnation, left me cold. In the mass, after all, Catholics claimed to have God physically present among them: one could even walk up to the communion rail and take a bite out of Him. The Protestants didn't even claim that much; so what, I wondered, was the point?

No, the organizer's path was not to be mine, and definitely not in the South, among either black or white.

But then what was? Writing was the one thing I had thought I knew how to do, before being struck dumb. But even it hardly presented a clear prospect: I was unknown and unpublished, except for the autumn dispatches to the Collegian in Colorado, and a more recent handful of poems.

Very well, then, how about leaving Selma and returning to graduate school and a profession?

Possibly, but in what? I had had enough of English; it had been impossible for me to sustain interest in Daniel Defoe's fiction in Atlanta almost a year earlier; and that was before the cataclysms of the Movement. I recall toying with the idea of law school, even to the point of taking a sample admission test; but in contrast to my previous superior performance on the SAT and GRE, my scores were not especially stellar; and in truth, the profession did not really grab me.

What, then, about religion? It interested me, no question, even more so after seeing the sides of it the movement had made visible. In Atlanta, and again with my walking partners at Camp Selma, I had looked into the programs of the Unitarian seminaries, including Harvard Divinity School.

But this notion presented problems too: if one were to become a religious professional, particularly a minister, shouldn't one at least be *religious?*

I wasn't, particularly, at that point. I felt rather like an avid but chair-bound baseball fan, able to reel off Jackie Robinson's batting average, but who couldn't hit a softball single or scoop up even the slowest grounder.

In sum, I was a walking specimen of early twenties self-doubt and alienation; Adjustment Reaction to Adulthood, indeed.

VII

Beyond my personal angst, the summer's general funk was deepened by the fact that around me the Selma movement was rapidly unraveling. The relief supplies in the basement of First Baptist had been corralled by a newcomer in town, one Elder William Ezra Greer. He became the overseer of something called SERF, the Selma Emergency Relief Fund. SERF itself, along with Greer's role in it, grew more ambiguous and less attractive as the summer went on. Greer traveled frequently up North, raising money which none of the rest of us could ever find out much about.

Even worse, as the rumors and suspicious talk spread around town, the established black leadership, especially Rev. F.D. Reese, President of the Dallas County Voters League, and his Vice President, a close-mouthed man named Ernest Doyle, reacted by attempting to suppress rather than resolve it.

Reese had acted heroically during the height of the movement; but in these dog days, his performance was pedestrian and increasingly self-serving. When questions and objections about SERF and the relief supplies were voiced in open meetings in the city's wards, they were ruled out of order, and it was soon announced that all ward meeting agendas would henceforth be controlled by the Voters League leadership. Furthermore, it was announced, the League executives would control any and all organized actions in the city.

Such high-handed tactics were hardly calculated to reassure the city's black citizens; But rather than sparking a revolt, the effect was to evoke their old habit of withdrawal and sullen apathy; the ward meetings soon dried up.

An insurgent exception was a preacher named Fairro Brown in the East Selma ward, who refused to knuckle under and stop raising questions about what was happening in SERF and why the Voters League continued to defend it. The leadership response was first, to tell him to shut up; and when he refused, to unilaterally abolish his ward organization and combine it with another, more pliable group.

Tish and I watched all this unfold with deepening apprehension. What was happening to this wonderful movement, with its inspiring oratory, magnificent singing, and bravery in the face of danger? Was it really degenerating into an undignified squabble over some bags of groceries and a few thousand dollars of charity? Were these leaders we had so recently revered turning into no more than ward heelers and petty political hustlers? How had this happened so fast? And where would it all end?

Since all the national staff had moved on, SCLC had sent a new local staff director for SCLC, Rev. Harold Middlebrook. Middlebrook was a young preacher from Tennessee, cocky but personable, and we liked him. He saw where things were headed, and spent a lot of time working quietly to persuade Reese and Doyle that they had to get rid of Elder Greer and clean up the SERF operation.

This housecleaning was necessary, he contended, to rebuild public confidence and be ready to take advantage of the Voting Rights Act. Middlebrook was thinking strategically and long term, looking beyond simply getting people registered, to making effective use of the franchise on behalf of a new progressive, and hopefully black city and county leadership. Sheriff Jim Clark would be up for re-election in 1966; he would be the movement's first target. And Mayor Smitherman would be next. To lay a meaningful foundation for this local revolution, the Voter's League's internal mess needed to be cleaned up, and soon.

But it wasn't; in fact, starting in late June, there was a series of new shocks, each more traumatic than the last.

VIII

First, on June 24, Elder Greer was arrested and charged with some euphemized version of seeking sex with underage girls and possessing pornography. All of which may have been true, but for Wilson Baker it was really only a pretext: his underlying goal was to question Greer closely about SERF and its connections with the Voters League leaders.

But before Baker had a chance to get down to business, Greer was bailed out of jail, by Ernest Doyle of the Voters League, who showed up along with the treasurer and counted out the $911 bond in cash.

As soon as Greer was out of jail, the DCVL leaders ordered him to pack his things, then drove him to the bus station. But just as the Greyhound was about to flap its door shut and head out of town, Baker's police appeared again and literally hauled Greer from his seat and back to the jail.

This second charge was a more serious one, that of making sexual advances to an underage girl, one of many daughters of a stalwart movement supporter. Before the movement, such goings on in the black community rarely merited the notice of white authorities; but this time it was different. And this time, Greer spent several days in jail, and as Wilson Baker told me later, he told his interrogators what they wanted to know. Greer was finally brought before a judge, fined $25, and sentenced to six months in jail. The sentence was suspended based on Greer's vow that he was leaving town, which he did.

Of course, Greer was mainly of interest to Baker for what he could tell about the doings of Rev. Reese and the DCVL leadership. And it seems that once back in stir, he gave Baker plenty of leads, which Baker assiduously followed up until, in early July, he had enough to take to the Dallas County grand jury. On July sixth, the grand jury indicted Reese on three counts of embezzlement, and he was arrested.

The amounts involved, by later standards, were paltry, hardly worth notice: three checks, for a total of $1850, which Reese had written on an account opened not long before in Montgomery, and used for a house payment and other personal items. The money belonged to DCVL, Baker's indictment alleged, and had been diverted and spent without authorization.

What remained of the Selma movement had been in public disarray ever since Greer's arrests. The DCVL leadership's attempt to spirit him out of town, followed by stonewalling of all internal questions, had produced angry calls for new elections in the body. These had been brushed aside by Reese and his cohorts. Now, with Reese in jail too, things really fell apart.

Tish and I were in the thick of this internal turmoil because we were SCLC staff, and SCLC was scrambling to salvage the situation in what had a few weeks ago been the capstone of its public achievements. Ralph Abernathy flew in and gave a stemwinding sermon to a packed but restive mass meeting, ridiculing the charges as a segregationist plot, urging them to stand behind Reese as their battle-tested local leader, and finally rousing them to a semblance of loyalty, if not enthusiasm.

Afterwards, Harold Middlebrook called Tish and me into a staff meeting where he informed us that an all-night canvass was starting, to drum up a huge crowd to greet Reese when he was released on bail the next day, and we were to be part of it.

Except that neither of us had the stomach for it. In the weeks leading up to the arrests, watching Reese and the others relentlessly undermining the very community structures which had made their rise possible, we had come to share the resentment of Fairro Brown and the other dissidents. By the time the indictments were announced, we were convinced it was time for a clean sweep and a new start. Abernathy's preaching had not persuaded us otherwise. We thought Middlebrook agreed with that view–or rather, that we agreed with him on it.

But now the SCLC line was one of loyalty. Whatever flaws Reese might have, he was their man, and they had resolved to stick with him. In retrospect, it is easy to see why: SCLC's leaders were southern black activists who had watched as many of their best and most promising leaders were either destroyed or silenced by similar efforts.

In fact, Dr. King himself had been charged with misusing funds not long after first coming to public notice in the Montgomery Bus Boycott. That had been a deliberate effort to abort his growth into a public figure whose challenges to the segregationist order were listened to around the world. It might have worked, too, except that King produced solid evidence to refute the charges.

That had been a close call – one of many – which he and those around him had never forgotten. They saw the same tactics now in play against Reese, and were not going to abandon him

As I say, this stance looks more plausible in hindsight. On the ground, at that moment, there was no way Tish and I could stomach working to build a show of support for a person and a local leadership we thought had betrayed and undermined the Selma movement. But when we told Middlebrook so, he reacted with cold fury: The policy decision had been made. Either we followed our orders and joined the canvass, he warned, or we would be fired.

We considered this, but only briefly, and repeated our refusal.

"All right then," Middlebrook snapped, "you're fired."

We went home in something of a state of shock. It was July of 1965 and we were in Selma, Alabama, a thousand miles and more away from any family or old friends, in a city where half the inhabitants considered us dangerous subversives; and we were cut loose, on our own, with little money and no prospects.

What were we going to do now?

IX

Fortunately for our sanity, we didn't have to wonder very long.

There was a crowd to meet Reese when he was bailed out the next day, but it was a sparse showing, less than a hundred, and perfunctory in its greeting. So much for the all-night blitz.

Late the next day the phone in our house rang, and it was

SCLC headquarters on the line. In a moment we were talking to Randolph Blackwell. He said that while the show of support for Reese had to go on as planned, he understood our scruples about it, and respected them. Thus if we were willing, he would override our dismissal by Middlebrook, and have us report directly to him in Atlanta. We accepted quickly, and with relief.

So we were back on the payroll; our $40 per week was safe. It wasn't much, even then; but it was all we had.

Not that I'm complaining about our wages; but for this pittance, we were doing – what?

Less and less, actually. The Selma movement was fragmented and adrift; hardly anything was left of Selma Free College; and I still wasn't writing dispatches for Atlanta. I guess the hope was that we could be of use when the Voting Rights bill finally passed. But it's not surprising that by the end of July, we were beginning to think the unthinkable, and look toward life beyond Selma and after the movement.

One important impetus to such consideration was the looming specter of Vietnam, and the reality of the military draft.

This distant war suddenly came home to us in midsummer. Mrs. Boynton was helping put two nieces through a boarding school in southern Alabama, and they spent some weeks of their vacation at the house. One of them, we discovered, had a boyfriend who was a couple years older.

We found this out when he showed up, in uniform, back for a brief respite from Vietnam. I don't recall his ever speaking a word to us, and not much more to anyone else. Mostly he just sat, in a dazed stupor, staring blankly at nothing we could see.

I wasn't sure if it was drugs or alcohol he was medicating himself with. But the sense of his having come out of something unutterably horrible, and being fated to return to it, was palpable. He stayed in the house for about three days, then was gone.

This glimpse of the war's human impact made the prospect of the draft more concrete. Even without such a reminder, it can truly be said that all American men of my generation had to steer the course of their young adulthood in large part in light of the demands of the Selective Service System, and I was no exception.

Since it's now been nearly thirty years since the draft was

ended, it may be worth mentioning how the system worked: On March 22, 1961, three months after my eighteenth birthday, I visited the draft board office in Cheyenne, Wyoming, where I was still in high school, and filled out a form. The form was put in a folder, which went into the board's filing cabinet, at the back. All over America, month by month, other new eighteen year-old males did the same thing. To fail to do so was a federal crime.

Likewise every month, Selective Service headquarters sent each local board a notice listing its quota – the number of draftees it was to send to the army. And in turn, a clerk at each board would open the file drawer, reach in and pull out a stack of the folders in the front section – representing the oldest among the draft-age males in its area.

The draft board then went through the stack, and classified the folders into various categories, as specified by law: A certain number were deemed IV-F, physically unfit, and exempted completely. Others would be deferred from consideration for a wide variety of reasons, the most common being that they were in college; these were classified as II-S. I had been classified II-S during my years at CSU, until the summer of 1964.

When all the files qualifying for deferments or exemptions had been laid aside, the oldest ones among those who were left were classified I-A; this meant they had been "selected" for military "service." Letters were sent summoning them to report for a military physical; and if they passed, they were inducted into the army for two years.

I was re-classified from II-S to I-A about the time I was setting out for Atlanta. But I hadn't worried about being drafted, because in 1965 there were still some exceptions to this rule. President Kennedy had, by executive order, directed that married men otherwise classified I-A, were not to be drafted. As a married man, I was covered. But after my Boston trip and the thunderbolt realization of my distrust for the official explanation of the Vietnam War, simply being deferred did not feel like enough for me. I sent off for some pamphlets that analyzed how the U.S. had become involved in Indochina, and everything I read reinforced my unease.

Besides which, for more than six months I had been enrolled in what amounted to a school of practical pacifist activism, and had as a mentor one of its most notable practitioners. I had heard about Gandhi, most importantly on that memorable evening when I ate Dr. King's dinner in jail; now I read about him, and about his influences, including Leo Tolstoy. I slogged through Tolstoy's book, *The Kingdom of God Is Within You*, which makes an eloquent case for radical pacifist anarchism.

Tolstoy was impressive, though I found I couldn't fully share his anarchist sentiments. What, I wondered, if the government wanted to draft me, not for the army but to work, say, in the Peace Corps, or some comparable program of domestic reconstruction? This was after all, when our government had also declared "war" on poverty, and such an effort seemed both desirable and practical. (I still think it is.) Would I be willing to be drafted for that? I decided my answer was yes.

That meant I was willing to live with some governmental coercion, so I wasn't much of an anarchist. But how much coercion, and for what purposes?

That was another matter. The more I looked at the nation's other, real war in Vietnam, the surer I was that I would not be willing to go there and fight.

But that was just one war, the latest in a long line. Other wars – notably World War II, had been generally judged righteous and worthwhile. Would I have wanted to opt out of them, too?

I might have, if it seemed there was another and better way. And after the experience of the movement, the notion of a nonviolent alternative to war seemed very real, and practical. We had played out the argument between violence and nonviolence on the streets of Selma, and the road to Montgomery; and in my eyes, nonviolence had won that argument, hands down.

No, I soon decided, there was no way I was going into the U.S. army, or any other military venture. So that made me – what?

Such an option had never been part of my consciousness before, so I had to hunt to find the right term: it made me a *conscientious objector.*

But what did that mean for the draft? If the term was new to me, it was familiar to others around SCLC, and someone said I could get more information from the Central Committee for Conscientious Objectors in Philadelphia. I ordered a of their

Handbook for Conscientious Objectors; it cost fifty cents.

When the book came, I studied it carefully. It was a new edition, only a couple of months old, and was very thorough in presenting the various possible options, from enlisting and asking for noncombatant status, to full non-cooperation and refusal of induction. It also talked about how to cope with the prison terms such intransigence was almost certain to produce.

I admired the draft resistance position, but knew I did not fully share it. Between these poles was the most common stance, that of a conscientious objector, who was expected to spend two years working in a government-approved job, as "alternative service" to the draft.

That fit me best, but the *Handbook* also cautioned that there was no guarantee of achieving this status. I had to apply for it, on a special government form, and be approved by my local draft board. Many local boards, it reported, were outright hostile to CO claims, legitimate or not. If refused, there was a series of appeals possible, before one wound up facing induction, and then the courts

The *Handbook* also explained that the current law permitted CO status only on the basis of "religious training and belief," involving a "supreme being." This was discouraging, because I couldn't affirm any such theological belief.

Then a few pages later, in a section brand new to that edition, I learned about the Supreme Court's Seeger decision of March 8, 1965. This was a major expansion of the law's reach, and one I might be able to fit into. When a notice came in mid-July from my board in Cheyenne, reaffirming my I-A status, I wrote back and requested the CO application form.

I wish I had kept a copy of the completed form, to be able to quote what I told the board. I know I was straightforward about my agnostic religious views, but still firm in rejecting participation in war, citing my Selma experience as the basis. And I tried to tell them, as politely as possible, that if they rejected my claim, I would be obliged to refuse induction.

I also know that when the form went into the mail, I figured the odds of ending up in jail were probably pretty high; and felt ready for that outcome. According to the *Handbook*, the typical sentence for draft refusal in early 1965 was a year and a day, and with time off for good behavior, about eight months actually behind bars. Such a stretch would not be fun; but I could get through it.

X

August was a tough month in Selma. The good news was that finally, on the sixth – Hiroshima day, and our first wedding anniversary – the Voting Rights Act was signed into law at the White House. Dr. King had called for federal registrars to be sent across the South, to supplant the systemic recalcitrance of local voting officials; but the Act didn't do this, allowing the appointment of special federal "referees" only in places where resistance had been especially flagrant. This was not a major drawback, though, because while the law permitted the local boards to continue, it left them with almost nothing to do.

A referee was appointed for Selma, of course, and registration there went smoothly. Actually, given the impact of the voting rights work there, going back long before the marches of the previous spring, by now many blacks in Dallas County were already registered. This day of Jubilee, then, was real but relatively subdued. It did not result in a sudden burst of new activity by SCLC staff, including us, because it wasn't really necessary. That was one measure of the breadth of the Movement's victory.

This was a good thing, too; because within a few days, after August 11, the mood of the American public was abruptly shifting, under the shock of black riots in the Watts section of Los Angeles. There had been racial outbreaks before; but the Watts "rebellion," as some militants termed it, represented a quantum leap in destruction. Selma remained calm, even torpid, as the news came in. But even from more than 2000 miles away, we could hear the echoes of the rioters' chants of "Burn, Baby, Burn!" and feel the earth moving under our feet.

The American public's support of new civil rights laws, we knew, was very fragile: it depended on the white majority being able to see blacks as noble victims, like the dignified marchers attacked by troopers at the foot of the Edmund Pettus bridge. Replace that image with one of club-wielding youths rampaging through nighttime streets, silhouetted against the glow of burning stores, smashing windows, and trading gunfire with police, and the cause was lost, wrecked like one of the overturned cars smoldering in L.A's nighttime streets.

Watts was soon followed by violence in our area, but of a different, more familiar sort. On August 20th, an Episcopal seminarian named Jonathan Daniels was shot down in broad daylight on the dusty streets of Hayneville, the seat of Lowndes County. The killer was a sometime deputy sheriff, Thomas Coleman.

I knew Daniels slightly. He had arrived in Selma in the winter, one of the hundreds of clergy who came to bear witness. But he had stayed on after the march, working with young people and folks in the countryside. Where I was the introverted townie, fretting over the Voters League's decline and my inability to write, Daniels was riding the rutted back roads in his little Volkswagen, visiting and talking with people. He was also sought out as a colleague by the continuing trickle of clergy who continued to pass through the city.

One of these latter-day pilgrims was Father Richard Morrisroe, a Catholic priest from Chicago. A week earlier, Daniels had taken Morrisroe with him to Hayneville, where they joined a small, mostly youthful march to the Lowndes County Courthouse, to protest the total exclusion of the black majority from the voting rolls.

Their march was peaceful enough, but it was also unprecedented in Lowndes, and the group was quickly arrested. It was after their release, into an empty courthouse square on a sun-baked afternoon, that the shooting started. Daniels walked with a group of the teenagers toward a local store. They weren't protesting now; they were looking for something cold to drink, and a telephone to call for a ride back to Selma.

Coleman was sitting on the porch of the store with a shotgun. Daniels saw him take aim, and his last act was to grab a couple of the youths in front of him and shove them out of the line of fire, taking the buckshot instead. In a moment he was dead in the dusty street. Behind him, Father Morrisroe also lay, bleeding and grievously wounded. Morrisroe lay there moaning for an hour before an ambulance came for him. He survived, but only after lengthy and extensive surgery.

This news was as shocking to us in Selma as Watts had been, and obviously closer to home. I heard later that Jim Clark was thrown into a state of panic by Daniels' murder, and gathered all available firepower to beat back what he foresaw as a mini-Watts black rampage. But nothing of the sort occurred; there was a funeral and a protest, but all was done peacefully and in order.

A contingent of national press returned for Daniels' memorial, and later for the trial of Tom Coleman in the Hayneville court house. There they saw an all-white jury reflexively uphold the region's hoary tradition. They accepted Coleman's claim that he thought Daniels was armed, and had shot him in self-defense, and acquitting him in short order. We were depressed by this outcome, but hardly surprised.

As the tension mingled with the heat, it was manifested in bizarre ways. We got a few phone calls with no one on the other end, just the sound of breathing. Then one afternoon, Tish and I came home to an empty house. Walking up the steps of the small porch, I saw a suitcase sitting by the low railing, out of sight of the sidewalk.

I was immediately on guard. Mrs. Boynton was away, We were not expecting any visitors. Why would a suitcase suddenly appear out of nowhere?

There had not been any racist bombings in Selma. But there had been dozens in Birmingham ("Bombingham," as it was sometimes called), and Dr. King's house in Montgomery had been bombed. Why not a bomb here?

Within a couple of minutes, I was in full-blown panic mode. Warning Tish to stay clear, I considered what to do. We couldn't go inside the house without finding out what was in that suitcase. But what if it was set to explode when opened? I walked back and forth in the small yard, uncertain what to do.

Finally I felt I had to chance it. Stepping by the low porch railing, I found that if I jumped with all my strength, I could reach over the rail and touch the suitcase. After several tries, I got a finger under one of the levers on its top. It snapped up, and I fell back to the grass, rolling away and covering my head.

Nothing. I tiptoed back, made another few jumps, managed to

snag the other latch, and rolled away again, head covered.

Again nothing. Going up the steps very gingerly, I saw the suitcase: open now, full of clothes. We closed it up again and went inside. It turned out to belong to an old friend of Mrs. Boynton, who had come to town unexpectedly.

Remembering the neatly folded women's clothes, I felt foolish about my panicked reaction. But not too foolish. After all, Mrs. Boynton was a prominent challenger of the status quo, and she was known to be sheltering us, two paid agitators. And four movement partisans in the area had already been killed by other means just that year.

So August was a tough month. It was also a time of transition for SCLC: After the Voting Rights Act, and after Watts, what was next for Dr. King, and SCLC? The movement had opened up the voting lists to southern blacks; but getting them signed up, and more important, mobilizing their votes for change–these were in the first place, a bureaucratic task, and in the second, a question of local politics. Neither of these was SCLC's forte. Dr. King and his circle were preachers, prophets– and impresarios of street theater. They had had a great run in Selma, as they had in Birmingham and elsewhere. What was to be their next production?

SCLC held its annual convention in Birmingham that month, but it was mostly sermons and banquets (plus *sotto voce* gossip about the fiascos of SCOPE), and didn't reveal much. Later on in August, we learned that in a few weeks there was to be an SCLC staff retreat in South Carolina, at Frogmore, a small Quaker retreat center. This sounded more like it; maybe there we could hear Dr. King and the others, out of the limelight, talk frankly about some of the many questions we had:

Where would the movement turn next? What issue would it take on? And what – I especially wanted to know now– about Vietnam? Dr. King was on record as a Christian pacifist, but he had said little in public about the war. Did his pacifism apply only to domestic issues?

None of these were merely theoretical questions. All of them could be rephrased into directly personal terms: Where was I going to go? What would I do there? And the draft aside, how would I deal with the rising tide of war? Tish and I arranged to ride along with Harold Middlebrook to the retreat, and counted down the days. I was also counting the days until a reply came from my draft board, though there was no deadline for that.

XI

Frogmore was an unpretentious place, in the coastal Carolina lowlands, with weathered stucco buildings surrounded by trees hung heavily with Spanish moss. At issue in the sessions was whether SCLC should turn its energies to the North, and specifically to Chicago. James Bevel, bouncing back from the failure of his late-spring Alabama plans, was now an enthusiastic supporter of the idea.

Dr. King was drawn toward Chicago as well, even though it involved taking on Chicago Mayor Richard J. Daley, one of the canniest politicians around. A band of activists there had invited Dr. King, and he saw that racism had sunk its tentacles deep into the life of the Windy City, as it had elsewhere in the North. Targeting Chicago had the additional advantage of surprise: the media were used to Dr. King working in the South; that was becoming old news. A nonviolent invasion of Chicago would be a new twist; and that was important.

By the time of Frogmore, the real internal debate was all but over: Dr. King was preparing to go to Chicago. But what I most remember about the retreat is a series of three unrelated events, one official, the second emphatically not, and the third entirely intangible, but perhaps the most revealing, at least to me.

The first was a comment by Dr. King at one of the sessions–perhaps it was no more than an aside in a longer discussion. He said that the war in Vietnam was becoming a major issue of our time, and that one day, he foresaw, his conscience would oblige him to speak out forcefully against it. But when he did so, he added, with a note of melancholy resignation, he, and by extension SCLC, would be made to pay for it, and pay heavily.

If this was a looming battle which Dr. King did not relish, neither did the rest of his staff, with the possible exception of Bevel. Vietnam, and all the conflicts and issues that were crowded under the umbrella term "foreign policy," were outside their turf.

A war is Asia was hard to relate to the concerns of their base communities for jobs, housing, schools, justice and respect; this was SCLC's bread and butter, and its pastoral focus. The staff might agree that terrible things were happening in Saigon; but between Saigon and Chicago, their preference was clear.

Dr. King, who had recently taken a beating in the press for making some mild comments about ending the war, had agreed that this was the only politically prudent course to follow. But it was also clear that this decision did not soothe his conscience, and it was easy to suspect that the debate was not over.

No one could blame the executive staff for wanting to steer clear of the quicksand Vietnam represented; I surely did not. And yet, Vietnam was already the troublesome uninvited guest at almost every American party, as it was to be for another ten years. It was already a constant irritant to my peace of mind. If SCLC was not going to address it, where could I find those who would?

The second important encounter came after a meeting, while we were all standing in line for a meal. I heard Bevel and Dr. King talking earnestly ahead of me, and tuned in, as by degrees, did most of the rest.

They were talking, debating about sex and marriage. How the topic came up, I don't know, but there they were. Bevel, in his tenor staccato, was making the case for what were known euphemistically as "open relationships," marriages in which the partners were explicitly allowed to seek sexual pleasure with others.

To this Dr. King sounded a baritone bass note of dissent. He had no faith in any such couplings, he said; the right way was the traditional one: monogamy and fidelity.

This was a friendly argument, like a college bull session; voices were not raised, no personal charges were hurled, and Dr. King did not attempt to pull rank. But it was still evident that their positions were deeply felt, and the colloquy was riveting to the listeners. Surely all of us present knew, by regular hearsay if not personal observation, that neither of these men was exactly a model of chastity. I would thus have expected Dr. King to go along with Bevel, at least to some extent, if only to provide himself with moral cover for what we all assumed was his habitual practice.

But no. Bevel argued skillfully: love was expansive;

possessiveness outmoded, and jealousy a bad habit. But Dr. King refused to budge: one man, one woman, forsaking all others–given the fallen state of human nature, that's the way it had to be. It was also what the Bible said.

Looking back, this exchange, finally interrupted by the arrival of the food, revealed a great deal. In Bevel there was the spirit of the times, pushing the limits and opening things up, trying to be ethically and situationally inclusive, and to see good in what he, and many others of the time, were doing. I don't recall if he did, but he could have parried Dr. King's biblical references with one of his own, the Apostle Paul from First Corinthians, proclaiming that "All things are lawful for me," a verse which conventional exegetes are anxious to diminish or ignore.

Dr. King, on the other hand, was tipping his hand as the more orthodox Christian: the standard is there, was his argument. He didn't say, but the implication was obvious, that his and our failures to live up to it didn't mean we should redraw the lines, but rather admit that we are sinners. We don't need new morals, was his point; we need the old remedies: forgiveness and grace.

Put into a gloss on their own, reputedly similar behavior, Bevel was insisting, "I'm not doing anything wrong," while Dr. King was admitting, "I am."

At the time, standing transfixed in that dinner line, I was mostly on Bevel's side, or at least I thought I was. A part of me still is, too; but time and my own misadventures have lately put me more in Dr. King's corner. Are all things really lawful to me? Maybe more than some people think should be; but even so, there are limits. And do I need grace and forgiveness? Do I need to breathe?

The third thing about the retreat was not immediately clear; I now imagine it coming into focus for me slowly afterward, on the long hot trip back across Georgia into Alabama. It was a sense of the truth of that enigmatic verse in the Gospel of John, 3:8, that the Spirit "is like the wind, and it blows where it wants to. And you hear the sound of it, but you don't know where it comes from, or where it is going."

Agnostic that I still was, I nevertheless had a strong sense of the presence and moving of something, for which the "spirit" was the best available name, as in one of our favorite Freedom songs:

"You Got to Do What the Spirit Say Do." By now there was no doubt in my mind that this Spirit had come to roost, like Noah's doves, above the low steeples of Brown Chapel eight months earlier, and it had hovered outside our often contentious staff meetings there as well. In those weeks, with this power somehow in our hands, the sense of the world, or at least one major portion of it, actually moving and shifting at our touch was almost palpable.

This was not, I knew even then, because of our superior virtue, though there surely was moral force in the lives of the black people of Selma at large. Nor was it the result of talent, though many in Dr. King's circle were greatly gifted. All our flawed strivings played their part, surely; but in and through them there was something more, something moving, something which made that place, that time, and us somehow more than ourselves, put us at the fulcrum of a larger play of forces, and enabled us to tip it in a constructive direction.

And now, riding away from Frogmore, I somehow felt –no, perceived–that this Spirit had moved on, blowing where it would. I couldn't explain why; but then again, there was really no need to. SCLC would surely mount other campaigns, in Chicago and who knew where else; and it might have more successes. Dr. King was still a man of greatness, with much to do, and much to give.

But now he, and we, and the movement itself were all shrinking somehow, deflating back to our normal human size, dealing with less exalted and more human concerns, issues and destinies. Whatever it was that moved "the movement," it seemed clear to me, was now moving on.

Was this intuition the deposit of all the summer's ambiguities? There had been the collapse of SCOPE; the Watts riot; the steady, distracting drumbeat of war. Closer to home were the SERF scandal, Rev. Reese's arrest, Jon Daniels' murder. And for me, the multiple absurdities of Selma Free College, the need to deal with the draft, and my own personal distress and need to find a clear personal direction.

They all played a part, I suppose; but then again, all of this was par for the course. None of it, and none of us, were really any more corrupt or fallible than we had been a year earlier. Maybe it was simply that a certain piece of work was done. The spirit blows where it will. Something was ending.

Whatever its source, hindsight bears out my perception: Selma did turn out to be the high-water mark of the civil rights movement; almost all afterwards was anti-climax and decline.

And what did this mean for Tish and me? We were increasingly clear that our time in Selma was drawing to a close, though we had no idea what was to follow.

Not long after we got back, an envelope came from my draft board. Holding it, I hesitated. Was the key to my future inside? What would it be? A round of appeals, followed by court appearances and a jail sentence? Or something else?

The letter was short and terse: My petition for Conscientious Objector status, Selective Service Classification I-O, was granted.

Chapter Seven
Finding a Voice Again

I

Why, I have long wondered, did my Cheyenne, Wyoming draft board grant me CO status without even insisting on a hearing?

There is one possibility that tantalizes: With the application, I was required to submit letters from three references, attesting to my sincerity. I can't recall who two of them were–probably friends or professors from Colorado State. But the third I have not forgotten: it was Dr. King.

I'm confident his secretary, Dora McDonald, wrote the letter, and probably signed it too; and I'm sure its content was boilerplate and platitudes; after all, what did Dr. King know about me? My name, and that I liked collard greens, at least in jail; but not much else. We had never talked about, say, war and peace.

Nonetheless, I have often seen the board in my mind's eye:

Middle-aged men, doubtless veterans of World War Two, with maybe one from Korea. Wyoming small businessmen or other local worthies. Democrats or Republicans, surely conservative in their basic sympathies, sitting around a table.

Brows furrowed as they passed around my file. A sigh escaped from one. A shaking of heads. They don't see many of these forms; Quakers, Mennonites and other religious dissenters were rare in southeastern Wyoming. I doubt they had yet heard of U.S. v. Seeger. At first glance, the reaction to the application was sharply negative.

But then they leafed through the reference letters. The one

148

from Atlanta stopped them.

Lips pursed. Eyes narrowed. One of them looked at another. "You thinkin' what I'm thinkin'?" said the one holding the file.

"Mebbe," said the other, who had already seen it. Then: "What I'm thinkin' is, do we need that one" – gesturing toward the Atlanta letter – "comin' to town for a trial?"

A nod.

Another sigh, then a look at the board clerk, who had heard about U.S. v. Seeger, and maybe explains about it. The upshot of which was that with decent lawyering I might well beat the rap.

Another sigh. "Nope," the chairman said, and the file slapped shut. "We don't need that."

I always emerge from the reverie smiling. It would have been big news in Cheyenne: Dr. Martin Luther King, Jr. coming to town, appearing as a character witness on behalf of an obscure draft refuser. It would have been worth risking a prison term.

II

Strictly speaking, the draft board's letter does not quite qualify as one of the nudges from Providence I've been looking for in this recollection. That's because I suspect much would have turned out the same whatever it had said: if it had rejected my claim, I had a good chance to win on appeal. But even if I had wound up in jail, there was likewise a good chance that some of the key connections I made later would still have come about.

That's barring disasters, of course: prison rape, riots, psychic breaks, any of a hundred possible contingencies.

Even so.

What comes closer to the mark than the board's action was my initial request – not the content so much as the timing. Because of the escalation of the Vietnam war, the government was rapidly increasing draft calls. Within weeks of my sending it, Lyndon Johnson rescinded the Kennedy order deferring married men.

When I heard this on the news, another image came to mind, and recurs with the memory: *An old black and white cartoon, with some slippery hero escaping the dungeon in the villain's castle. He races toward the gate and freedom. But as he streaks across the courtyard, the villain appears in the window above and shouts to the guards: "Lower the portcullis–don't let him get away!" Big chains rattle, huge wooden pulleys squeal and a barred gate, with sharp points at the bottom, plummets toward the ground. The hero has to bend low and wiggle to barely squeeze under, just before the heavy bars crash into the dirt and the gate is slammed shut forever.*

When my petition was mailed, I was still deferred, so there was no question that, however benighted, I was acting in good faith. But the gate was coming down, and once it shut, the scene at the board would, I am sure, been quite different. Did they know about the impending change? I doubt it.

III

In a way I felt released by the conclusion that the Spirit that had animated the movement had moved on. I must have, because not long after our return from Frogmore, mirabile dictu–I felt an idea taking form, and with it an increasing urge to write. And when I put paper in the typewriter, what appeared there was not a poem, but that old friend, prose:

"As the leader of the Negro struggle for equality," it began, "Martin Luther King is faced with the perils of success. His movement, it is now clear, is going to bring America's Negroes into the mainstream of national life. It will not be done "NOW!" or even within a generation, but the forces set in motion by five years of mass nonviolent effort are too far-reaching to be reversed."

But despite this achievement, it noted, ". . . the Negro leadership – with Dr. King as its symbol – seems uncertain about what to do next. There is a strong temptation to dig in, to consolidate and expand the gains already made; in short, to begin playing the political game for an ever larger piece of the national pie, as did the labor movement at the end of its rise.

"Such a feeling," it acknowledged, "is natural. 'Freedom Now!' translated into more specific terms means for most Negroes simply: 'We want in!' Into the economy, into the political circuses, into all the currents and eddies of the American mainstream."

This may be enough for the rank and file. But: "The way is not so clear for Dr. King, primarily because during his entire career his whole stance has been not merely an economic one but more basically a *moral* one. He opposed segregation not simply because it was economically debilitating but because it was *evil* – and unchristian."

But now, I wrote, echoing Dr. King's own ruminations in South Carolina, this moral stance "stands revealed as a two-edged sword, because many of the moral issues which Dr. King and the movement have raised in the restricted context of the segregated south have national and international contexts and implications as well. With the entry of the civil rights movement into the level of full national participation, the leaders are no longer just confronting the nation with its regional sins but are themselves confronted – as full-fledged citizens and moral spokesmen – with the issues of over-all national policy.

"The most unsettling context for these issues is, of course, the war in Vietnam. Negro leaders, even up to last spring in Selma, frequently told draft-age males in their audiences that they had no business fighting for anything abroad until things were straightened out at home. Now, faced with the realities of tripled draft calls and Negro bodies being shipped home from southeast Asia, many are wishing they had kept their mouths shut."

It was too late for that now. I scorned "The traditional Uncle Tom leadership," which "hastily scrambled aboard the Johnson escalator . . ." but noted that "the militants, and Dr. King as the most successful and articulate of them all, were thrown into a public quandary."

The resulting confusion was all too visible. "Dr. King is not known as a man of vacillation, yet his statements on the war seem curiously circumspect, almost tame. His staff is said to be deeply, even bitterly divided over strategy regarding a response to the war. Some have reportedly urged him to begin immediately an all-out effort to challenge the surrounding smokescreen of official double talk. Others are convinced that such a course is suicide; they contend that Dr. King and his organization would be red-baited into bankruptcy and oblivion even within the Negro community. The few mild protests he has made are said already to have cut substantially into the donations coming into his Atlanta office. Given the permanently precarious finances of civil rights organizations, this makes further ventures even more risky.

"At present Dr. King seems to be trying to walk a tortuous middle path: opposing the war as a matter of form but doing so as quietly as possible. . . . Perhaps Dr. King is biding his time, hoping to get his campaign against northern slums off the ground before tackling the broader issues of the war. There is something to be said for this as a matter of tactics."

"It is also possible, however, that Dr. King simply doesn't yet know what to do. Challenging the war would mean an open break with the administration and the loss of all the perquisites of membership in the 'great consensus.'"

But despite feeling sympathy for this vulnerability, the thrust of my concern was clear:

"In any case it seems unlikely that he can continue to be quiet in the face of continuing escalation of the fighting without seriously compromising his acknowledged role as a man of principle.

Further, I didn't think a course of open dissent would be as isolating as he feared:

"Though going through motions of support, the nation is clearly uneasy about the war. This self-conscious, almost guilty attitude is new in the national consciousness, and Dr. King's nonviolent campaigns can take much credit for its development. As the administration's facade of 'national honor' in Vietnam continues to be punctured by the responsible press, the underlying contradictions and moral evasions of our policy are brought home ever more forcefully to much of the informed public. Each new lapse of credibility, each new revelation of official immorality cries out the louder for rebuke and makes more critical the need for authentic moral challenge to the war.

"Among all our truly national figures Dr. King is one of the few who are undeniably men of conscience. If there is to be any significant national reassessment of the Vietnam war and the politics it exemplifies, he could do more than anyone else to bring this about – and his implicit acquiescence in the war would do the most to prevent any such reassessment."

Saying this once was not enough:

"He cannot escape these facts\. No one thrust as Dr. King has been onto the stage of world attention and conflict can ever again find a refuge in the sectional or minority cause from which he sprang. When he accepted the Nobel peace prize he baptized all races into his congregation and confirmed the world as the battleground for his gospel of nonviolence and reconciliation. He is no longer – and probably never again can be – a spokesman for just an American Negro minority. Simply because of his position in the world limelight, he cannot avoid confrontation with the ethical implications of national and international events.

"This is why– as the Johnson administration talks of escalating the war beyond 450,000 men, of bombing Hanoi-Haiphong and even of confronting China on the Asian mainland – the virtual silence of the unchallenged spokesman of American conscience becomes ever louder and more painful to those who have followed him thus far."

The closing reached for rhetorical sweep:

"The war in Vietnam is perhaps the gravest challenge of Dr. King's career – and conceivably its culmination. Who among us could blame him if, faced with this dilemma, he agonizes over his course of action? No one, surely; but Martin Luther King, Jr. is not only answerable to us of today: he must also walk with history as well. And if in his agony he should fail to act, it must be asked: could history forgive him?"

IV

The title was "Dilemma for Dr. King." It was, in a way, a letter to him, a way of picking up on the aside at Frogmore about Vietnam, and putting in my two cents worth.

Reading it now, the prose, despite tinges of purple, seems competent enough. More important, the analysis was correct and the forecast prescient:

Within a year Dr. King had concluded he had to take a firm, high-profile stand against the war. When he did, he was indeed red-baited, both by the administration and some of his most important supporters. Yet the power of his witness, combined with the continuing horror of the war, soon brought many of them back to his side. And the struggle against the war and what produced it was the culmination of his career.

Reading over these few typed sheets in the room at Mrs. Boynton's house, the best thing about it was simply that it said what I felt needed to be said. If it could get published, the issue would be joined in public. And I knew where I wanted to send it first: The *Christian Century*.

I recalled seeing copies of the magazine somewhere, maybe in SCLC's office, maybe in some other staffer's pocket. As the major liberal Protestant weekly, a staunch supporter of the movement, it was a journal Dr. King was likely to keep up with. And I sensed that Dr. King would be involved in an ongoing debate over this issue, mostly out of my sight, and for that matter maybe primarily within his own mind and heart. If he read my piece somewhere, or heard about it from someone whose views he respected, maybe it could nudge him along.

Whatever impact it might have on its target, though, the piece was much more important to me. Above all, it meant my writing voice had finally returned. I felt a bit like Zacharias in the gospel of Luke, struck dumb until the birth to John the Baptist, once the child was born, and he could speak again.

Besides, looking at it now, almost four decades later, I can see in it the seed of much of my work as a writer ever since: a preoccupation with religion and how it affects the world and vice versa. From one angle this can look like journalism, from another a preliminary to history; and from yet another, perhaps the least appealing, sheer punditry and editorializing; and my work has been all of these things. Sometimes, at its best, it has also been a force for discernment, that carried its own influence, helping move situations forward.

V

Anyway, I was pleased with the piece, and soon had it in the mail to the *Christian Century*'s office in Chicago. Not long afterward, Tish and I were also headed out of town, back toward New York and New England. Invited again by people we had met during the frenzied weeks of March, we were happy to get away. After the Frogmore retreat and my CO approval, our focus was shifting rapidly to post-Selma thinking. While the war had become the lodestar for my social concern, SCLC's local focus was increasingly on Selma and Dallas County politics. Besides, as a now-certified CO, I still owed the government two years of work, and needed to find an acceptable job to meet the obligation. So we were also prospecting.

One jibe often tossed at white northerners in the movement was that we were really just tourists, getting our jollies at the expense of black people, before heading home to show our slides to the folks at home, and start looking for the next new thing.

I could make a pretty good case then as to why this charge didn't apply to us: for one thing, we weren't going back home; we didn't know where we were headed, and we had no trust fund or wealthy benefactors waiting to take us in. For another, we would soon have to leave town anyway, as part of the consequences of acts of conscience we had been led to by being in the movement; and besides, we agreed with the burgeoning sentiment that it was up to black people to run their own struggle.

All true. But not the whole truth.

We were also tired of Selma. It was a small town, a long way from anywhere we were interested in, with few possibilities for work, education, or even a break from the racial-cultural polarization which defined so much of its life. Perhaps these were the reactions of movement tourists. But we could have added, defensively, that you didn't have to be white, middle class and from out of town to reach this conclusion: black Selmians had been voting thus with their feet for decades, heading North at the first opportunity, as they had been leaving much of the South.

And we were burned out on the movement. The internal jockeying, as we had seen, could be brutal. The sexual politics, even from the sidelines, were exhausting. And there was no future for us in it anyway.

This reaction was not the same thing as disillusionment. I've waded through enough curdled testaments of ex-sixties turncoats to want to make that crystal clear. Sure the personal failings of our colleagues, including Dr. King, could and did wear them, and us, out. But nothing I have seen adds up to even a molehill besides his greatness, sealed with the violent death he expected and accepted. The same goes for the movement as we knew it.

Furthermore, the sense remained that somehow the motley crew I had stumbled into had served as a vehicle of something better and higher. The whole had added up to more than the sum of its parts, and almost despite itself made its society a better place. This conviction was not gone then, and still remains. The chorus of those who would have our children and grandchildren believe that we were part of a "destructive generation," (the title of a particularly egregious screed by David Horowitz and Peter Collier) will get no echo from my voice. I was honored to have been a part of it, and still am.

Nevertheless, as we traveled north in the fall of 1965, I was tired of it, and it was time for a change. It was a good thing too: on this trip, we began to learn how quickly the media page turns. When we arrived at Yale, for instance, we were last year's news; there was still a place to stay and some welcoming, apologetic hosts; but the VIP quarters were otherwise engaged, and the interested crowds were somewhere else. I didn't really mind; we were, after all, moving on ourselves.

Then it was on to Boston, where we had another amusing and ironic media experience: In late spring, Dr. King had addressed the Massachusetts legislature, and we had read brief reports about it in Alabama newspapers. In the articles, King was quoted as repeating what we were learning were some of his stock rhetorical phrases. He had a large repertory of these, which he knitted together in various combinations for his audiences.

Now in Massachusetts, we read that Dr. King was making several stops in Alabama, and the article quoted him as repeating exactly the same phrases down there. The echoes made me smile. Maybe we were getting too familiar with the movement, and the artifice that inevitably went with it.

It was a good, if quiet trip, but one thing that didn't turn up en route was a solid lead for a job. I wasn't too worried about this. The CO Handbook said that if all else failed, the government would find work for me; and I was pretty much prepared to let them do that and take potluck.

Tish had a different view: she wanted to be somewhere interesting, away from the boondocks, and in particular a place with access to an affordable college in which to resume her work for a degree. This made sense, but I still wasn't taking much positive action to that end.

My lazy and lackadaisical approach to the future was becoming an issue for us; fortunately, though, Providence was ready to knock on the door and bail me out.

VI

And that is indeed how it happened: with a knock at the door of the house on Lapsley Street.

Mrs. Boynton was out, and I was busy. Tish went to the door, but with some trepidation. We were still wary of strangers; and when she opened the door, she gasped and jumped back: there stood a strange young white woman.

The stranger, however, was just as shocked to see Tish. But when she spoke, stammering something apologetic about being in the wrong place, her lack of a southern accent was reassuring. This was not, it seemed, a local come to terrorize the Yankee invaders.

The stranger, likewise reassured by Tish's accent, explained that she was canvassing the neighborhood in search of any black citizens who might not yet be registered to vote. She added that she was part of a group of college students visiting Selma on a study trip through the South.

Intrigued now, Tish invited her in. The visitor was part of the very first class at Friends World College. It was a new experimental college, based on Long Island, not far from New York City, and was connected with Quakers.

Quakers? Now Tish was fascinated. She had heard or read something about Quakers awhile back, and had written off to Philadelphia for some brochures about them. I hadn't paid much attention, except to the fact that they were supposed to be one of the pillars of religious pacifism; I thought there might have been some connection between them and CCCO, since both had Philadelphia addresses.

Once started, the visitor talked animatedly about both Quakers and their Friends World College: her family was Quaker; the school was a radical and exciting experiment. They didn't take courses as such; instead they studied world problems, and weighed possible solutions in the field.

And they traveled, to put faces on ideas and test concepts in the real world. This trip was to the South; but later in the spring they'd be leaving for Europe. After that, term by term, they would make their way around the world, ending up back on Long Island to complete their degrees and proceed to change the world.

By now Tish was spellbound, and the two talked on and on until the visitor realized she was late for rejoining her group. Tish invited her to bring the whole group back for more talk later.

When I came in, Tish was still bubbling with excitement. Besides the fascinating details about the school, she had mentioned that I was a CO, and the visitor recognized the term–in fact, said they had COs on their faculty, doing alternative service there, and was sure they'd want to meet me. Tish smelled the possibility of a job, and Long Island was about as far away from the boondocks as we could hope to get.

Sure enough, that evening the whole group showed up, crammed into a Volkswagen Microbus. They were led by Arthur Meyer, the school's Assistant Director. We all sat around and talked up a storm, hitting it off.

And Tish had guessed right: Meyer was very interested in my CO status, my need for a job, and (though he didn't say so then) the fact that people in my position were accustomed to working cheap. They were leaving town shortly, Meyer said, but he would pass my name on to the Director, one Morris Mitchell, back in Long Island.

V

Was this Providence? Quakerism is one of the key elements of the future I would have chosen had I been able to. But there were only a handful of Quakers in all of Alabama and Mississippi, and none lived within many miles of Dallas County. Yet a Quaker knocked at my door, and brought a job with her.

After that day had started the process, it seemed to go like clockwork: I wrote to Morris Mitchell, and he responded, inviting me to apply for a junior faculty position there.

Me? A college faculty member? After my failed try at a pottery class, I didn't even have a degree. But my movement experience fit Mitchell's problem-centered theory of education. Besides, I wouldn't actually be teaching courses – the job was more like being a camp counselor and driver. My CO status was also an asset for a Quaker school; and I was accustomed to the low pay which was all they could offer.

Before Christmas a job offer came, to begin in February, 1966, at Friends World College's home campus, preparing for the arrival of the second class. I accepted gladly, and my draft board in Cheyenne, relieved of further paperwork, approved it without a blink.

I also had something else: A letter from the *Christian Century*, accepting "Dilemma for Dr. King" for publication.

By now we were all but done in Selma. But there was one last ticket to be punched: my old Camp Selma cellmate, Ira Blalock, had written, asking for us to come visit, courtesy of his Unitarian church in Portland, Oregon. At that point Greyhound was offering unlimited bus tickets, ninety-nine days of travel for ninety-nine dollars. We set up a long looping itinerary which included stops in San Francisco to see Jim and some of the alumni of Selma Free College, as well as Tish's relatives in Marin County.

We were on buses for more than seven grueling days altogether; I can still smell the oily plastic odor that gets into your skin after more than a few hours on the bus. But we were glad to do it. And we were not back in Selma more that a couple of weeks before, in early February, 1966, we packed up our still meager belongings and climbed onto a train in Montgomery that was to take us to New York.

VII

One of my first and most vivid images of my new home came two days later, heading east from Manhattan. The VW Microbus carrying us came up out of the Midtown Tunnel, headed east across Queens, and then drove abruptly over a rise, into the biggest cemetery I had ever seen. The headstones spread out for what seemed like miles on either side of us, their irregular ranks covering the hillocks and hollows all the way to the close horizon. Welcome to New York.

Harrow Hill was a large Long Island estate that had been given to Friends World College as a headquarters, at least until it could be sold and a proper campus established. After breakfast the next morning, with butterflies in my stomach, I set out to meet my boss, the distinguished scholar and educational philosopher, Dr. Morris Mitchell.

I walked down an ornate hallway and knocked at the door of a parlor that had been turned into an office.

When the door opened, I had to look up to meet the eyes of its occupant. Morris Mitchell was a very tall man, still powerful and towering at the age of seventy-one. White hair, piercing eyes, and a strong, firm grip.

"How do you do, Dr. Mitchell," I began, "I'm–

"Don't call me Dr. Mitchell," he said, turning back toward his desk, which was strewn with papers. I immediately caught his southern twang, softened by many years in northern exile, but still distinct.

"Call me Morris," he continued, sinking into his chair. "I'm a Quaker, and Quakers don't hold with titles. I don't even want to be called 'Mister.' 'Mister' comes from 'Master,' and I acknowledge no man as my master and don't want to be master of anyone else."

I stood there, dumbfounded but captivated, my mouth open. This next chapter, I knew at once, was going to be something very special.

But that's another story.

After Shocks

I

Five months later, in June of 1966, we were back in Selma. But this time, we were indeed movement tourists: I was driving a VW bus with half a dozen Friends World College students in tow; Tish was riding shotgun.

"Dilemma for Dr. King" had been published, in the March 16 issue of the *Christian Century*. It was an obscure debut, toward the back of the issue; and made more so by a grim stroke of fate: The magazine's founding editor, Charles Clayton Morrison, had died the week before. His black-bordered photo took up the entire front page, displacing the usual listing of article headlines, where I had hoped for a bit of exposure. Did Dr. King ever see it?

But never mind. I was now a published author. They had even paid me $35; I still have the framed stub of that check. I kept a notebook handy as we traveled, and was alert to future article topics.

I was also becoming a Quaker. That process deserves a book of its own, but the short version is simply that like the right-size shoe, it fit.

We were on a weeks-long study trip. Already we had eaten pecans at Koinonia Farm in Americus, Georgia; we had seen the dams of the Tennessee Valley Authority, which were one of Morris Mitchell's most – and our least – favorite educational projects.

But Tennessee had its consolations. Near Knoxville, we had spent the night at the Highlander Center, the pioneering integrated study center. Dr. King's one visit there had been immortalized on billboards across the South as proof of his ties to a "Communist Training School." But in truth, Dr. King had not found communism at Highlander; he found something more significant to his movement: Mrs. Septima Clark. It was at Highlander that she developed her quietly subversive Citizenship Education Program.

And now Selma. We were taking the progressive version of a regional grand tour. This was a long way from ROTC in Colorado.

By this time voter registration in Dallas County was pretty much a done deal, except around the edges. Already a political campaign was underway, in which the new black voters were keenly interested and would play a decisive role: Sheriff Jim Clark was up for re-election, and Wilson Baker was running against him.

By rights there should have been a black candidate for sheriff; there was a black majority in the county. But the local black leadership was still too fragmented and quarrelsome to unite behind a single figure. Considering the field, I recalled James Bevel telling a mass meeting about "studying my white folks," and it didn't take much study to figure out that Baker would be better for blacks.

Since SCLC was nonprofit and officially nonpartisan, it was not involved directly in the campaign. The office, moreover, had moved, from downtown to a house in one of older corners of Selma's small black middle class area. The space was, we understood, being shared with SNCC. We drove up and I knocked on the door.

A young black man whom I did not know answered, and reluctantly invited us in. He had an Afro hairdo, still a new item on the scene, and a surly expression. He told us that Septima Clark was working with the office, but she was busy at the moment.

Shortly the students were sitting in a circle, and he obligingly led us in a couple of freedom songs, and then answered a few questions about Selma. When asked about the movement, though, he launched into a diatribe against the white power structure.

I knew the black nationalist tide in the movement had been rising rapidly. Just a few months earlier, SNCC had sent its last few white staffers packing. But it was still a surprise to hear such talk on what was presumably SCLC turf. He went on about how the white man had oppressed his people long enough, and that they were going to rise up and demand what was rightfully theirs, no matter what, and by any means necessary. His tone got more and more hostile, and my students' expressions increasingly glum.

After several moments of this, and as he worked himself into what seemed like a frenzy of righteous rage, I glanced to one side and saw that Mrs. Clark had come from elsewhere in the house and was standing quietly in a doorway, unseen by our host-antagonist, listening.

Her hair was longer than I remembered it from that interview so long ago in Atlanta, combed out; but the flowered dress was similar, as was her erect carriage and serious expression.

The harangue climbed to new heights of accusation and threat; a long pointed finger stabbed now at the air, now at us, making the students shrink away guiltily. As it continued, Mrs. Clark began to frown.

And then, just as the young man was reaching for some kind of punishing peroration, calling down doom upon all the accursed low-melanine hordes, she spoke.

Quietly.

"All right now," she said. "I think that's enough of that."

He stopped in mid-jab. The inflated rhetorical outrage, and the exaggerated body language that went with it, both vanished instantly, like a pricked balloon.

He stooped a bit, said "Yes ma'am," sounding like an obedient six-year old, and shuffled silently away.

Did the students realize that in those few moments they had gotten most of their tuition money's worth? I don't know; but they did.